Thorstein Veblen and the Institutionalists

Thorstein Veblen and the Institutionalists

A Study in the Social Philosophy of Economics

David Seckler

with a Foreword by
Lord Robbins

The London School of Economics
and Political Science

COLORADO ASSOCIATED UNIVERSITY PRESS
Boulder, Colorado

First published in the United States 1975 by
COLORADO ASSOCIATED UNIVERSITY PRESS
1424 Fifteenth Street, Boulder, CO. 80302

ISBN: 87081–055–3

Library of Congress Card Catalog Number 73–91642

Printed in Great Britain

TO FRANK

Contents

Foreword

The place of institutionalism in the history of economic thought is a matter of some perplexity. That the term itself served as a war-cry congenial to quite a number of muddled and slightly disturbed spirits is clear enough. At the time of its publication in the twenties, the volume entitled *The Trend of Economics* (edited by Rexford Guy Tugwell), which, so far as it had any unity at all, was a sort of manifesto of such dissidence, had an enormous *réclame* until it was quietly and courteously deflated by a masterly essay by Allyn Young.* Nowadays I doubt whether five per cent of the younger generation of economists have even heard of it – which perhaps only shows that, as forecasters, its practitioners signally failed to deliver the goods. As for any influence or progress on the lines indicated, it must be admitted that it has been negligible.

Nevertheless, in its day, the so-called movement was not unimportant. It attracted at least the nominal adherence or support of a few great men, Mitchell and J. M. Clark for instance; and, if only negatively, it evoked useful clarification of mainstream economic thinking – if it had only given rise to Young's review and the essay by Frank Knight entitled *The Limitations of Scientific Method in Economics*, itself embodied in the symposium, it would have served some purpose. But what it really was all about is still very difficult to describe shortly. As Professor Seckler shows in this valuable monograph, it is possible greatly to overemphasize – as I used to do – any very direct continuity with the somewhat similar but much more important Historical School in Germany and elsewhere. As he also shows, apart from a common antipathy to the classical or neoclassical tradition, it is not at all easy to detect any consensus of subject-matter or even method among those who were prepared to accept the designation. As one reads the various declarations of dissent and intention, one is inevitably reminded of

* Reprinted in his *Economic Problems: New and Old* (New York, 1927).

the classic quotation from *Alice in Wonderland* of which, in quite
another context, Dennis Robertson made such effective use. 'She's
in that state of mind,' said the White Queen, 'that she wants to
deny something – only she doesn't know what to deny!'

Apart from this frame of mind, however, they all shared one
common characteristic – intense admiration for the work of Thorstein Veblen. And this brings us to a subject of much greater
interest. For whatever view may ultimately be taken of Veblen's
positive contribution, there can surely be no doubt either of his
importance as an influence or, in some sense or other, the quality
of his thought. Those elaborate sentences with their burlesque
polysyllabic jargon and their biting sarcasm must certainly be
regarded as part of the important *literature* of our time, whether
or not one agrees with the correctness of the perspective or the
fairness of the judgement; and their author must be taken seriously.

Unfortunately the logical and scientific contents of Veblen's
work, as distinct from its qualities as stimulus and satire, are much
more difficult to assess and identify. It is the burden of Professor
Seckler's highly penetrating, but very sympathetic, analysis that,
intellectually, Veblen was a split personality. One side of him was
attracted, as a moth to a candle, to the idea of economics as
objective generalization in the strict sense of the natural sciences,
explaining everything in terms of the discernible behaviour of
collectives, with 'stage' theories and impressionistic generalizations about groups, all tailored to his particular, often very brilliant, intentions. On the other hand he was much too clever to be
really taken in by the naïve pseudo-explanations of pure
Behaviourism; and there is another side of his work which Professor Seckler not unjustly describes as standing in the tradition –
how Veblen would have hated the classification – of Radical
Humanism, in which collective social phenomena are traced back
to individual motivation with mind as an operative entity. And so,
more often than not, because of these contradictions, the result is
something which, however provocative as thought and infectious
emotion, makes no easily describable contribution to the total of
logically coherent, not to say testable ideas. As Professor Seckler,
himself the most sympathetic and gentle of surgeons, remarks:
'There are in fact two Veblens. There is the behaviouristic Veblen
and the humanistic Veblen inextricably intertwined to the extent

that any theory of Veblen based in the one or the other interpretation can be directly contradicted with a quotation – usually in the same piece – arguing to the contrary.'

It is the merit of Professor Seckler's book that it sorts out all these difficulties and puts them in proper perspective. It is not an exhaustive history of Institutionalism – how dreary and voluminous that would be – but rather a broad survey of the main hisstorical influences and intellectual issues involved. He provides a useful account of the background of the so-called movement; a vivid presentation and analysis of Veblen's central position without the tedious summaries of successive publications so frequent in surveys of this kind; and brief discussions of the contribution, or lack of contribution, of the various leading figures influenced, or claiming to be influenced, in some way or other by Veblen. He has no great sympathy for all the followers, although he presents a charming picture of Wesley Mitchell who, despite some statements of unbelievable naïveté, was, needless to say, too considerable a figure to be fairly classified mainly under any sectarian designation. But, as he confesses in his introduction, Veblen has had a lifelong fascination for him; and if in the end the verdict is adverse, to the extent quoted above, it is still a verdict of considerable admiration rather than denigration of any kind other than purely logical.

As Professor Seckler explains in his Preface, his book began years ago as a doctor's thesis. But let no one think that it has that complexion now. Professor Seckler carries his learning lightly; and while every paragraph involves a weight of erudition concealed behind it, the result of his revisions and omissions is eminently readable. Indeed it is so readable that my only fear for it would be that, for that very reason, it may be too lightly discussed by the not inconsiderable number of contemporary academics who equate readability with superficiality and regard no contribution as deserving of respect unless it is at once overloaded with material superfluous to the argument and a positive bore to plough through. In my judgment, however, Professor Seckler has made not only a significant contribution to the history of thought but also, what after all should be the main purpose of such work if it is to be more than mere documentation, a contribution which is itself a stimulus to further thinking.

ROBBINS

Preface

This book is the result of what can only be reasonably described as a lifelong obsession with Veblen. Oddly enough, I can remember as though it were yesterday the exact moment my interest began. One of my chores as a boy was taking the 'clinkers' out of the coal furnace every night. I remember thinking, while engaged in this odious occupation, something like a quarter of a century ago, of a very curious title I had accidentally run across; it was *The Theory of the Leisure Class*. Intrigued by this title, I got the book and read at it. I have been so reading at it ever since and, although it has had an enormous impact on my thought and life (for years I lived in an excessive degree of penury, partly so as not to 'conspicuously consume' – a deprivation for which I now compensate myself), I cannot really aver that I have read all of it yet. Certainly, if I have, it has been by means of random bombardment – for unlike any of Veblen's other works, I never could read it from start to finish. Why, I do not know.

The story continues through another accident. I went to the University of Denver where there were, as far as I could tell, only two professors – one in history, the other J. Fagg Foster, who was and is a confirmed institutional economist. Foster is a former student of C. E. Ayres, who represents a wing of institutionalism I strongly reject. But Foster also knows Veblen through and through. He put me through the paces of Veblenian philosophy.

Then another word-accident occurred. I had heard of the London School of Economics and was intrigued by the fact that such a famous centre of learning would be so humble as to call itself a mere school. Accordingly, I decided to quit the University of Denver – I think in my junior year – and enrol in this mysterious institution. I arrived in London but was too distracted by that wonderful city to find the object of my pursuit.

I returned to Denver and, after obtaining the master's degree, applied to L.S.E.; and since my interests were in the history of economic thought, I was assigned to Lionel (now Lord) Robbins.

This was an interesting event because Robbins' classic *Essay on the Nature and Significance of Economic Science* epitomized, in the eyes of the institutionalists, everything that was wrong with economics, and I was an ardent institutionalist!

I eventually decided that I could do no better than write a thesis on institutionalism under the direction of this most famous opponent. (I believe I secretly hoped, in my naïveté, to convert him!) I shall not discuss the impact of this great man, other than to say that Lord Robbins gently encouraged me to read the works of Karl R. Popper (I shall never forget his shock when I had to ask him to spell the name!) and Friedrich von Hayek.

With these names – Veblen, Foster, Robbins, Popper and Hayek – the story of the background of this book is complete.

It has been a long time since the original manuscript was filed as a Ph.D. dissertation at L.S.E. in 1959 and, I am happy to say, it has changed considerably since then. I have worked on it, on and off, more or less continuously ever since. If I have not completely deciphered what Graham Wallas aptly called the 'Secret of Veblen', I have at least discovered why he has been an obsession to me. Veblen was himself obsessed by the ancient problem of freedom – of 'free will versus determinism' – and so am I.

I am grateful to many people for help in writing this book over the long years it evolved. First, of course, Lord Robbins' kind advice and patient reading of (it seems) a near-infinite series of drafts is paramount. I learned much from the lectures given at L.S.E. by Professors Popper and Agassi – and more yet from Popper's published works. Fagg Foster and I still disagree over institutionalism, but I have profited greatly from our disagreement. Joseph Dorfman kindly read an earlier version of the manuscript and caught a shockingly large number of errors of detail – and, I fear, several may survive. I also doubt if Professor Dorfman would agree on the interpretation of institutionalism theory presented here, but, again, I owe much to him. Finally, Friedrich von Hayek read an earlier draft of Chapter 7 and found, I am proud to say, that (with the exception of some material on Freud, which has since been excised) it met with his good approval.

I wish to thank the copyright-holders (named in brackets) who have kindly given permission for the use of copyright material: *American Economic Review*, Supplement (Mar 1928) (American

Economic Association); C. E. Ayres, *The Theory of Economic Progress* (University of North Carolina Press, 1944); Joseph Dorfman, *Thorstein Veblen and His America* (Copyright 1934, Copyright © renewed 1962 by Joseph Dorfman, reprinted by permission of The Viking Press, Inc.); Chandler Morse (ed.), *Fact and Theory in Economics: The Testament of an Institutionalist: Collected Papers of Morris A. Copeland* (© 1958 by Cornell University, used by permission of Cornell University Press); John Rogers Commons, *Myself* and *The Legal Foundations of Capitalism* (Mrs Anne Commons Polisar); Lucy Sprague Mitchell, *Two Lives: The Story of Wesley Clair Mitchell and Myself* (Copyright © 1953 by Lucy Sprague Mitchell, reprinted by permission of McIntosh & Otis, Inc. and Simon & Schuster); 'Thorstein Veblen: Some Neglected Points in the Theory of Socialism' from November 1891 issue of *Annals of the American Academy of Political and Social Science* (A.A.P.S.S.); Thorstein Veblen, 'On the Intellectual Pre-eminence of the Jews in Modern Europe' (*Political Science Quarterly*, xxxiv (Mar 1919)); Thorstein Veblen, 'The Socialist Economics of Karl Marx and His Followers' (*Quarterly Journal of Economics* (Aug 1906 and Feb 1907)); Thorstein Veblen, 'The Limitations of Marginal Utility', *Journal of Political Economy*, xvii, No. 9 (Nov 1909) and 'The Place of Science in Modern Civilization', *American Journal of Sociology*, xi (Mar 1906) (University of Chicago Press).

The publishers have made every effort to trace the copyright-holders but if they have inadvertently overlooked any, they will be pleased to make the necessary arrangement at the first opportunity.

DAVID SECKLER

Fort Collins, Colorado
September 1973

1 Introduction

A certain air of dismay has crept into contemporary economics.[1] Joan Robinson is one of the more eminent and vociferous critics of the present state of the science. John Kenneth Galbraith has publicly protested at the unreceptiveness of the profession to his ideas. The development of mathematical and statistical methods which carried the profession on a crest of excitement for two decades after the war now appears to many to be but another exercise in intellectual sterility. Young 'radical' economists are protesting at the lack of relevance and meaning of economics in contemporary society. Most alarming perhaps is circumstantial evidence of the quiet exodus of serious and imaginative young people out of economics into other disciplines and professions.

These current attitudes provide a fitting backdrop to a study of Thorstein Veblen and the school of institutional economics. Not only did institutionalism arise out of an essentially similar milieu in the first two decades of this century, but its platform of protest against what may be called the mainstream economics of its day was very similar to contemporary complaints.

The institutionalists protested at the overly abstract and deductive character of mainstream economics. They wished to make economics more 'relevant' to social problems and employ it as an instrument of reform. They thought that economics was hopelessly mixed in utilitarianism and that no real progress could occur until this archaic utilitarian view of man was replaced by a modern interpretation based on the findings of contemporary philosophy, psychology and anthropology. Above all, the institutionalists wished to provide economics with a criterion of value other than the price of commodities. They wanted to distinguish between right and wrong, production and exploitation. They were concerned with economists' preoccupation with the perfectly competitive model and free trade while the world was becoming dominated by big business and imperialism. They emphasized the impact of technology on society and the force of legal and social institutions in determining human choices. Some were even prepared to reject, in their more sanguine moments, the very means of thought of mainstream economists and complimented themselves on their personal use of non-Aristotelian logic.

All this has a strikingly familiar ring. Other than for the prose style (in most cases far superior), some of the half-century-old institutionalist works sound like the latest revelations of the contemporary underground in economics. This is particularly true of Thorstein Veblen. Yet Veblen is hardly a current folk hero. Indeed, his status has not changed in the twenty years since Albert Einstein observed '. . . the American economist Thorstein Veblen . . . [is] one of the most remarkable political writers not only in America but in the entire world. . . . It seems a great pity that this great man is not sufficiently appreciated in his own country.'[2]

Part of the reason for the neglect of Veblen is his peculiar style of writing. He wrote very long sentences in a highly satirical vein. The ability to comprehend the one and to enjoy the other is not a notable characteristic of the young radical. But this is certainly not the whole answer to the problem. Many people eminently qualified in both respects have a hard time understanding Veblen. Almost every one admits he is some kind of genius – but hard to understand.

Graham Wallas exemplified this reaction. In a review of Veblen's *Imperial Germany*, Wallas said that while Veblen is clearly a genius, he wished 'someone would write a "Secret of Veblen", summing up (with an index!) the four books which have so far appeared'.[3]

Veblen himself noticed the problem. In the one instance where he replied to a critic – to John Cummings' very critical review of *The Theory of the Leisure Class* – Veblen observed that his prose seemed to arouse in the reader 'something of an inflection of sadness, such as argues a profound solicitude together with a baffled endeavor to find that the diction employed expresses any meaning whatever.'[4] Cummings later recanted, 'I have often wondered how I could have been so blind.'[5]

Part of the objective of this study is to provide at least part of that 'secret' Wallas intuitively sensed in Veblen's works. Veblen is perfectly understandable within a certain context. Outside that context his basic thinking appears confused and contradictory, which, indeed, it was.

Confusion is compounded in turning from Veblen the individual to the school of institutionalism. There is little controversy over who the major institutionalists *are*, but a great deal of uncertainty regarding what precisely institutionalism *is*. This peculiar circumstance may be illustrated in terms of Schumpeter's description of the Ricardian school of economics: '... the group was a genuine school in one sense: there was one master, one doctrine, personal coherence; there was a core; there were zones of influence; there were fringe ends.'[6]

In institutionalism there was not one but three 'masters' – Thorstein Veblen, John R. Commons and Wesley C. Mitchell.

There was a 'core' among whom some of the better-known names are J. M. Clarke, Clarence E. Ayres, Morris A. Copeland, Rexford G. Tugwell, Walton N. Hamilton, John S. Gambs, Allen C. Gruchy, A. D. Wolfe and Walter W. Stewart.

Certainly there were personal coherence, zones of influence and fringe ends. Simon Kuznets, John Galbraith, Arthur Burns and T. W. Schultz fit in one or the other of these categories.

One thing is apparent in this listing: institutionalism has been a remarkably fecund source to the pinnacles of American economists. In the above listing there is one Nobel laureate in economics and several past presidents of the American Economic Association. Veblen was offered the presidency, but he refused.

In terms of these criteria there can be no doubt that institutionalism was a genuine school. But there is the additional and all-important criterion of 'one doctrine' in Schumpeter's definition, and it is with respect to this that the question becomes confused. As Paul T. Homan has observed:

> ... the numerous proponents of the institutional approach to economics differ so markedly in their views concerning the purpose, content and methodology of institutional economics and the bonds of spiritual unity between them, engaged as they are in diverse and vaguely related tasks, are so intangible that the use of the term 'school' is justified only if the loosest possible meaning is attached to it.[7]

J. M. Clarke considered such early figures as Adam Smith, John Stuart Mill and Henry Sidgwick institutionalists. Wesley

Mitchell often spoke approvingly of economists who made 'excursions into institutional economics'.[8] Yet Mitchell sharply criticized John R. Commons for his definition of institutional economics as simply the attempt to give 'collective action ... its due place in economic theory'.[9]

There has always been this controversy over whether institutional economics is merely a subject-matter within economics – the study of economic institutions – or a true 'ism', in Schumpeter's sense 'a genuine school'. If it is just a subject-matter, it is of little theoretic interest; if it is a doctrine, then clearly some economists are institutionalists and others are not.

In reaction to the subject-matter definition, Paul T. Homan decided that Veblen was really the *only* institutionalist.[10] Then, as though to exhaust all permutations, D. R. Scott declared that 'Veblen [is] not an Institutionalist'.[11]

It is little wonder that the chapters on 'institutionalism' are uniformly the weakest chapters in any standard text in the history of economic thought. Eric Roll, for example, concludes his chapter on institutionalism with a paragraph, the last sentence of which directly contradicts the first:

> Even if one were to accept the interpretation that Veblen's chief legacy is an emphasis upon statistical studies, one could yet point out that Veblen's own writings were almost wholly theoretical. ... On the other hand, as Veblen's own work so well shows, nothing worthwhile has ever been achieved in any science by a perpetual amassing of facts without the guidance of theory.[12]

Perhaps Joseph Schumpeter could have sorted all this out in his *magnum opus, History of Economic Analysis*, but, interestingly enough, he postponed writing the institutionalist chapter to the last, and his untimely death left it uncompleted. Whatever Schumpeter might have said in this unfinished chapter, one thing is certain: he would not have accepted the subject-matter approach to institutionalism. He would have insisted on 'one doctrine', as he did with other schools of thought, and had he found no doctrine particularly institutionalist, he would have considered 'institutionalism' a misnomer and the effort to establish this school a failure.

Institutionalism is in fact a set of doctrines, each reasonably consistent within itself, but incompatible with the others. This is one essential clue in unravelling the mystery of institutionalism. It is not 'a genuine school', but rather a set of schools very loosely amalgamated by a common subject-matter.

Institutionalism is divided into two great wings superficially united by a common interest in institutions but doctrinally separated by the antipodal minds and personalities of Veblen and Commons. Veblen was a rarefied intellectual, a literary 'figure', a man whose feel for logical and aesthetic form drove him to distraction. Commons was something of a country bumpkin, never really at home in the intellectual world, a man devoid of the concept of form to a really remarkable degree. On the other hand, Veblen's very asceticism rendered him incompetent in the world of affairs. He was at heart a revolutionary, but was aesthetically unable to relate to any group of real people. Commons was the academic activist *par excellence*. He is probably responsible for more actual reform – more legislative enactments – than any academician before or since. No two men could be more different than Veblen and Commons, and they accordingly attracted very different disciples. The Veblen wing pursued doctrinal refinement of the master's works to, at times, ludicrous extremes. The Commons wing abandoned all doctrines – as did their master – in favour of a rough-and-ready eclecticism in which successful reform became the test of validity.

These two wings thus constitute a peculiar ménage of antipodal types. Both wings centred in the end on institutions: Veblenians because of the role of institutions in the grand march of history; the followers of Commons because of institutions as obstacles and instruments of reform. But here the relationship basically ends. Doctrinally speaking, the relationship between the two is no more substantial than, as Veblen observed in another respect, that 'between a saw horse and a real horse'.

Of course, only a few of the later institutionalists were consistent disciples of either Veblen or Commons. Most were intellectually reared in both traditions and in the tradition of mainstream economics as well. Herein lies the source of the remarkable impact of institutionalism on the development of many of America's greatest economists. Young men were challenged by its revolutionary overtones. They got a sense of the sweep of history and the depths of philosophy from Veblen. They were imbued with

reformist zeal in the tradition of Commons. Yet most attended
universities where institutionalism was a minority discipline.
This not only heightened its appeal as an underground movement, it also meant that these young people had a thorough
grounding in mainstream economics. What better training for
a budding economist? And what a tragedy that it is now mostly
gone.

The first step in deciphering the mystery of institutionalist
doctrine is, then, recognition of the two separate wings established
by Veblen and Commons. But this is only a first step. Veblen himself was torn between two doctrines and, indeed, the conflict
within his own mind was more severe, epistemologically speaking,
than that between Commons and himself. One of these Veblenian
variations created yet another, if minor, complication in the form
of Wesley C. Mitchell.

Mitchell was Veblen's favourite student and a sometime
admirer of Commons. He was simultaneously a great student of
the history and practice of mainstream economics. Thus, Mitchell
stands in the first instance as a cardinal representative of those
beneficial influences just mentioned and he is commonly acknowledged to be one of the greatest American economists.

Mitchell was one of the first serious practitioners of quantitative
economics. Through his monumental study of *Business Cycles*,
through the influence of his students, and through the creation of
the National Bureau of Economic Research, Mitchell became one
of the founding fathers of quantitative economics. Strangely
enough, Mitchell was directly inspired to quantitative work by
Veblen, whose own works employed facts largely for purposes of
amusement. Yet Veblen was privately an avid – even compulsive
– fact-gatherer. He has been described as 'the last man who knew
everything',[13] and at the University of Missouri he taught a course
in quantitative methods!

However, the spin-off of quantitative economics from institutionalism is little more than a historical curiosity. Quantitative
economics soon lost its institutionalist origins and has become
rather the epitome of that rarefied and distant intellectual tendency that so many institutionalists despised. Indeed, a case could
be made that modern econometrics, with its almost exclusive
preoccupation with statistical methodology, is an altogether different thing from the quantitative methods envisaged by Mitchell

and brought to its finest fruition in the works of his student, Simon Kuznets.

The ultimate complication in institutionalist doctrine occurs in the works of the ultimately complicated Thorstein Veblen. There is no doubt that Veblen spent his entire intellectual life employing two mutually contradictory theories.

Veblen's formative years in the last quarter of the nineteenth century were a period of extraordinary ferment in social philosophy. The philosophical implications of the Darwinian revolution were beginning to be felt in force. Herbert Spencer in England and William Graham Sumner in America were energetically reconstructing social philosophy in the image of this grand biological conception. The period was strikingly similar to the revolution in social philosophy sparked by Newtonian physics a century before. As Newtonian physics created the classical economics of Adam Smith and his successors, many inclined to believe that Darwinian biology would create the new economics.

Veblen was especially influenced by this historic challenge because of a remarkable accident: his father sent him to Carleton College as a young man because Carleton was the nearest school. J. B. Clark, the finest classical economist in America, happened to be teaching there and taught young Veblen all there was to know of mainstream economics. Then Veblen proceeded to Yale and studied social philosophy under William Graham Sumner! It is no wonder that the first methodological article Veblen published asked 'Why is Economics not an Evolutionary Science?'[14]

In this brilliant article, Veblen contended that economics was incapable of becoming a true science because of its methodological presuppositions. It assumes man to be a rationalistic, choosing individual attempting to maximize his well-being. Given this assumption, Veblen said, economics is reduced to a mere exercise in empathy. All it can do is attempt to guess what such a man would do by deductive logic designed to simulate his (alleged) mental processes. With these premises, Veblen said, economics is 'teleological', 'taxonomic' and 'tautological' – in a word, all that genuine evolutionary science is not.

Veblen proposed reconstructing the economic image of man on Darwinian grounds. Like other biological phenomena, he said, man is the end-product of long historical processes of selection over which he has little, if any, control. He is caught in an institutional and cultural web, handed down through habits and institutions from generation to generation, subject to change through such exogenous forces as war, famine, disease, or the expansion of technology. In this construction, man as a free, choosing agent drops out of the equation and the way is clear for a true 'science' of man. Veblen was driven by this methodological imperative. As he cogently put it, 'the method of sufficient reason' characteristic of the old economics should be replaced by 'the method of efficient cause' followed by other sciences.

This methodological imperative has a highly familiar ring in contemporary social science. It is precisely the methodological platform of behaviourism from the time of J. B. Watson through B. F. Skinner's latest pronouncement aptly entitled *Beyond Freedom and Dignity*. Veblen could fairly be considered the first methodological behaviourist.[15]

But he would renounce the title. Veblen was never able to overcome the essentially humanistic view of classical economics. He was unable consistently to follow his own methodological prescriptions, partly because of his own good sense and partly because he discovered a fundamental epistemological flaw in the theory of behaviourism. Again, he was among the first to discover this problem although it has since been rediscovered by others. Thus, while Veblen the methodologist may have regarded humanism as merely a vulgar kind of anthropomorphism, methodologically unacceptable to a true science of man, Veblen the logician found humanism *logically necessary*. And Veblen was above all a logician.

In this respect one might say of Veblen, as Keynes said in a memorable passage of Edgeworth, that he 'knew that he was skating on thin ice; and as life went on his love of skating and his distrust of the ice increased, by a malicious fate, *pari passu*'.[16]

Thus the third complication. Not only are there two very distinct wings of institutionalism between Commons and Veblen and yet a third in the quantitative traditional of Mitchell, but there are in fact two Veblens. There is the behaviouristic Veblen and the humanistic Veblen inextricably intertwined to the extent that any theory of Veblen based on one or the other interpretation can be directly contradicted with a quotation – usually in the same piece – arguing to the contrary. Herein lies the source of that mysterious elusiveness that so many have detected in Veblen's work. Herein lies as well the reason why institutionalism never became a proper school. The Commons wing never had a doctrine and the Veblen wing was schizophrenically torn between mutually exclusive doctrines. There was no consistent doctrine.

Before proceeding to the details of Veblen and the institutionalists, the reader should be forewarned of a rather peculiar detour in the text. This is Chapter 7 entitled 'Radical Individualism'. It is not specifically about the institutionalists at all but rather about the social philosophy of a different school of thought associated pre-eminently with the work of Karl Menger, Friedrich von Hayek, Karl Popper and Lord Robbins. Why this apparent *divertissement*?

The reason is this: at roughly the same time as Veblen was labouring to create a behaviouristic solution to certain cardinal questions of social philosophy, Karl Menger was labouring to create an essentially humanistic solution to these same questions. Thus, by following out the Menger tradition of radical individualism, one can obtain a better grasp of what Veblen himself – in his humanistic inclinations – was trying to achieve. Veblen was driven to behaviourism because he felt that humanism could not adequately address certain cardinal questions of social philosophy. Menger and his followers tried to solve these same questions within the context of humanism. In so far as humanism is successful, behaviourism is a red herring; that is the eventual conclusion of this study.

In sum, institutionalism has always been something of a mystery in the history of economic thought. It has never held together as a 'school', and the writings of Veblen – its greatest mind – have baffled even the most perceptive analysts. The essential clue to deciphering institutionalism is to recognize that it is not one but a set of doctrines. There is the essentially historical-school approach of Commons and his disciples (see Chapters 2 and 9 below). There is the quantitative economics of Mitchell and his followers which often became confused with the preachings of the historical school. Finally, there is the ultimately complicated Veblen himself, torn between two mutually exclusive theories, inextricably tangled in both through the course of his life. The students of these three masters (and four doctrines) naturally grew into a virtual cornucopia of combinations and permutations of the basic themes. Some became Veblenian purists pursuing his methodological prescriptions into behaviourism. Others, following the lead of Commons or Mitchell, delved into the detailed study of institutions or of statistics, depending on their individual proclivities, to the exclusion of theory. Others more or less gave up on institutionalism and became famous economists in the mainstream.

All this contrary development fragmented the school and dispersed its people to the point where it has basically died out. Yet one cannot but feel that the course of American economics benefited from the institutionalist experience. It failed as a revolutionary doctrine, but succeeded perhaps as a reformist movement. Many of the best American economists of today would not be what they are had it not been for institutionalism, and perhaps with the contemporary press for reform in mainstream economics, institutionalism may still have a role to play. No matter how one regards it, as a historical curiosity or as a guide to the future development of economics, it is at the very least an intriguing intellectual puzzle; and, quite possibly, an avenue to discovery.

2 Prelude to Institutionalism

Institutionalism properly began in 1898 with the publication of Veblen's article entitled 'Why is Economics not an Evolutionary Science?' As noted in the Introduction, this article levelled the basic institutionalist complaints against mainstream economics and formulated the institutionalist prospectus of reform. Within a year Veblen published a longer article in three parts, with substantially the same message, entitled 'The Preconceptions of Economic Science'.[1] Together these two papers 'compelled a whole generation of economists to search their hearts lest the truth be not in them'.[2]

In order to appreciate the impact of these two papers on the profession, it is necessary to obtain a perspective on the state of American economics at the time. For American economics was then greatly agitated by the changes and programmes of yet another revolutionary doctrine – the German historical school, or *Historismus*.[3] The conjuncture of institutionalism with *Historismus*, together with the then internal struggle within the mainstream over the use of marginal analysis, created a volatile situation among whose many consequences was a hopeless confusion over the meaning and intent of institutionalism itself.

Historismus began in the 1860s and 1870s with the works of Wilhelm Roscher and reached its apex around 1900 with the later work of Gustav Schmoller. In the course of these thirty or forty years, the historical school gained the support of such eminent German economists as Bruno Hildebrand, Johannes Conrad and Karl Knies, and soon came to dominate German economic thought. The story of the German historical movement is a story of its own. Its course turns and twists with each successive figure in the school; at many times differences between various members within the school, for example between the 'old historical school' and the 'new historical school', appear greater than those between the historical school, *per se*, and its opposition. But at least in the

Schmoller rendition, the deductive methods of classical economics were to be replaced by the methods of induction. Facts were to precede interpretations, generalizations were to emerge only from the brick-by-brick accumulation of empirical data. Schmoller exercised virtually absolute control over appointments to influential university posts, and under his influence work in the graduate schools at Berlin, Halle and Heidelberg became historical monographs or inquiries into problems of federal and municipal administration and similar empirical studies – to the consequent detriment of theory.

The programme of the German historical school sparked a very complex, bitter and personal battle between Schmoller and representatives of the mainstream, particularly Karl Menger and Eugen von Böhm-Bawerk of the Austrian school of economics. This battle – the famous *Methodenstreit*, over induction and deduction – drew the question out of narrowly economic circles into more general ideas of epistemology, of the meaning of history, the relativity of knowledge; the settled sands of old philosophic systems were stirred.[4]

The question of *Historismus* is as complex as that of institutionalism itself, and, fortunately, it is not necessary for this inquiry to go into the inextricably tangled doctrinal convolutions of that Germanic development. All that is of interest here is the suspicion that there is a direct line of descent from this early German development to institutionalism vis-à-vis the early American historical school. If this contention is true, then the influence of the American historical school upon institutionalism should be readily apparent from an examination of the persons, doctrines and policies of the American historical school itself. It is the short but turbulent history of this American historical school, therefore, that is of major interest.

In the two decades following the Civil War, the study of political economy in America truly resembled the 'dismal science'. It was perhaps not so dismal in its conclusions as in its actual pursuit. The faculties of the universities were peopled largely with ecclesiastics. The course in political economy was generally taught by the president or the chancellor of the university, and his qualifications lay more often than not solely in the realm of piety. Political economy, resting upon the self-evident formulations found in the popular textbooks, such as Millicent Garrett Fawcett's *Political*

Economy for Beginners, were used as illustrative material for lectures demonstrating the Infinite Wisdom of the Creator and the Harmony of the Universe. A substantial goal of education was to train competent ministers of the faith and devoted laity for the congregations. In this respect, a trustee of Carleton College (Veblen's *alma mater*) spoke for all when he said:

> This Christian college is ever our ally, as we seek to combat the superficial scepticism, or coarse but taking infidelity, or vulgar vice. . . . In it therefore, Moses comes before Socrates, David before Homer, Paul before Plato and Jesus Christ is acknowledged Lord of all.[5]

In the American study of political economy, extreme *laissez-faire* dogma exceeded that known in the most conservative circles of Europe and became, indeed, almost a theology in itself. Rigorous adherence to its dogma was 'not made the test of economic orthodoxy, merely. It was used to decide whether a man was an economist at all.'[6] However, around the 1880s there is discernible the beginnings of a reaction against this tradition. Part of the reaction was doubtless spurred by a growing sense of what Veblen would have called 'aesthetic nausea'. Another part of the reaction was prompted by an increasingly apparent discrepancy between the conclusions of political economy and the demands of economic policy.

At this time, fragments of the German historical discussion were beginning to appear on the American scene, largely through the American edition of Roscher's *Principles of Political Economy.* Many pedagogues seized on the historical movement as a possible way out of their predicament by using it to amend the traditional doctrine.[7] William Watts Folwell, one of the first Americans to speak approvingly of the historical doctrine, clearly illustrates this strange bifurcation of aims in the interests of compromise:

> The next and first thing of such a [political economy] course proper, is to draw a line of separation between political economy and national [historical school-type] economy and to relegate to the latter a considerable body of vexatious, practical questions, such as the tariff, the greenback, and transportation problems . . . this separation is believed to be essential to the unembarrassed consideration of theoretical and scientific

questions on the one hand and, on the other, to the handling of practical problems in legislation and society. It is thus rendered possible for a teacher of political economy to consent to practical measures of national economy which find their justification quite outside of his science.[8]

Encouraged by such a prospect, an increasing number of the American professors of political economy recommended to their better students postgraduate work in Germany under the auspices of the historical school. Thus, F. W. Taussig, F. A. Fetter, J. B. Clark, R. T. Ely, S. N. Patten, E. R. A. Seligman and others received a first-hand introduction to *Historismus* and its teachers.

Many of these young men returned to America imbued with the spirit of *Historismus* and inspired by the example of Knies, Conrad and Schmoller. They were determined to break the 'crust', as Ely put it, which had formed over American political economy. The vehicle for their attack was to be a formal association of the younger economists. E. J. James and S. N. Patten launched the Society for the Study of National Economy. The programme of the Society consisted of little more than an ardent advocation of state intervention in various social problems – education, conservation, labour conflicts and the like.[9] This narrow declaration of aims failed to attract the interest of a sufficient number of subscribers, and the plans for the Society soon collapsed. The lack of response to this initial programme encouraged Ely to push forward a bolder plan.

Ely's plan, with the active support of Henry Carter Adams and E. R. A. Seligman, resulted in the first meeting of the American Economic Association in 1885. The meeting was attended by most of the German-trained economists and also by many in a more traditional position in economic theory. It was realized that if the Association were to be a success, it must not be simply an association of the more radical elements but must also attract the support of a large portion of the more conservative economists. Consequently, Ely's particular plan[10] was submitted only as a 'provisional programme', a point of departure for discussion, and not as an ultimate statement of aims. In discussions of Ely's proposals, many statements were made that provide some insight into the very heterogeneous composition of this meeting. Most of the members agree with J. B. Clark's view of Ely's programme:

'... the point upon which individuals will be unable to unite is, especially, the strong condemnation of the "laissez-faire" doctrine.'[11] And they were apprehensive lest others would think that by rejecting extreme *laissez-faire*, they were advocating the 'German political system' which was, in their view, 'equally erroneous'.[12] Patten adamantly condemned the over-emphasis on induction as a method in the social sciences.[13] And they all (Ely included!) expressed deep concern that some might think this association an expression of the aims and methods of the German historical school.[14] After the discussion, the task of designing a suitable programme was referred to committee.

The ensuing statement of principles modified Ely's original views and was, as he noted, 'a compromise on behalf of catholicity':[15]

1. We regard the state as an agency whose positive assistance is one of the indispensable conditions of human progress.

2. We believe that political economy as a science is still in an early stage of development. While we appreciate the work of former economists, we look not so much to speculation as to the historical and statistical study of actual conditions of economic life for the satisfactory accomplishment of that development.

3. We hold that the conflict of labour and capital has brought into prominence a vast number of social problems, whose solution requires the united efforts, each in its own sphere, of the church, of the state and of science.

4. In the study of the industrial and commercial policy of governments we take no partisan attitude. We believe in a progressive development of economic conditions, which must be met by a corresponding development of legislative policy.[16]

The protestations of Ely and others to the contrary, there is little doubt but that even this watered-down version of the basic principles displays a strong bent towards *Historismus*. It was recognized as such by the more traditional members of the Association, and they wished to emphasize that even this comparatively timid platform was simply a general statement, not binding on individual members. Article II of the Constitution of this association is again reminiscent of the aims of the historical school. It provides, among other things, that the Association should encourage '. . . economic research, especially the historical and statistical study of the actual conditions of industrial life'.[17] 'The following topics are suggested to the chairman of the standing committees, as fit and proper subjects for reports:

1. Effect of Half-Time Working on the Labourer.
2. The Normal Working Day.
3. Employment of Women in Factories.
4. Municipal Finance.
5. The Income from Public Works in Cities.
6. Rent in the United States.
7. National Railroad Commission.
8. Limitation of Suffrage as a Remedy for Abuses in Local Administration.
9. Effect of Transport on the Worker.
10. The Silver Question.'[18]

But the Constitution of the Association, and even the discussion leading to its formulation, do not give an adequate picture of the historical programme as received in America. In these discussions, the statements of the new school were necessarily tempered by considerations of policy and their real views conditioned by the overriding desire to establish an association of economists as a going concern.

In order to obtain an adequate appreciation of the full extent and range of this school, it is therefore necessary to look for material not fashioned under the constraint of compromise. Soon after the meeting at Saratoga, the editor of the magazine *Science* invited some of the members of the younger school to debate the issues with other economists in its pages. The essays contributed by Ely, Richmond Mayo-Smith, Adams and Seligman, and the critical replies by Taussig and others, were subsequently reprinted as the *Science Economic Discussion*.[19] These essays give a clear, uninhibited statement of the programme and postulates of the historical school in America. Three major positions were outlined:

(1) The state is of paramount importance in the actual conduct of industrial life; it thus deserves a place in economic analysis as a basic factor of production. In the words of E. J. James:

There is no more significant difference between what, for lack of better terms, we may call the old and the new schools of political economy than their respective attitudes toward the state . . . the nature of its service is just as fundamental to production as that of labour or capital. . . . It is a fundamental economic category.[20]

Ely assumed the most extreme view in this regard; he said that the new school 'places society above the individual, because the whole is more than any of its parts', and endorsed the idea that all the forces of the community should be placed '. . . at command for the accomplishment of a life-aim in accordance with notions of benevolence'.[21]

(2) As the history of a culture unfolds, the changing composition of the culture amounts not only to a change in degree, but to a fundamental change in kind. Each generation must, therefore, reformulate the interpretation of economic reality. Adams expressed this proposition in the following terms: '. . . the law of its [society's] own development is the only permanent and universal fact which its analysis discloses: all other facts are relative truths; and those systems of thought based upon them temporary systems'.[22] Ely later described this idea of the relativity of knowledge as one of the 'fundamental things in our minds'.[23]

(3) In order to account fully for these basic changes in society, in order to keep theoretical speculations in date with cultural changes, induction must predominate over deduction in the formulation of economic knowledge. This tenet of the new school must not be confused with the weaker position that observation and deduction 'go hand in hand' or even that observation is 'more important' than deduction. In this case, the word 'induction' is used in its precise logical reference, namely as a method of generalization from specific facts to general laws based upon objective similarities and differences in the facts alone. As Ely said, 'The inductive political economist . . . gathers together particular facts . . . and observing particulars in which these facts agree among themselves, separate out these similars and form what we call generalization.'[24]

These three major propositions constitute the core of the *Discussion*. All the protagonists – Ely, Smith, Adams and Seligman – state the same content in different terminology. These propositions are comprehensive in the sense that what else is discussed are either ill-formulated expressions of primarily propaganda content, or plain *obiter dicta* peculiar to each author. There can be little doubt that, at this stage, the new school in American political economy was little more than the German historical school incarnate.[25]

Considering the firm grip the historical school had on the minds of these young economists in the 1880s, the confidence with which these doctrines were advocated, and near messianic faith in an impending revolution in the study of political economy, it is astonishing to see how rapidly it collapsed. By 1890 the American historical school was largely a dead letter. As Frank A. Fetter observed, 'Certainly the years from 1885 on belong to the utility value theorists. . . . This sudden revival of abstracter or deductive economics, just as such studies seemed to be growing into discredit, is one of the remarkable chapters in economic theory.'[26]

There are several reasons for this sudden demise.

One reason is, as Fetter observes, the exciting new development of marginal analysis or, as he put it, 'utility value' theory. Many of the German-trained economists – J. M. Clark, Taussig and Fetter are the outstanding examples – seized on these new theoretical developments and became eminent members of the mainstream in economics. Another reason was a real need to break the crust that had formed over the old economics. Consequently the infiltration of German literature and influence was welcomed even among the old guard as a much-needed respite from the suffocating influence of the traditional theory. Yet the older economists, W. W. Folwell, Bernard Moses, C. F. Dunbar, J. Laurence Laughlin, were unwilling to abandon the traditional heritage completely. The problem was to find a balance between the old and the new – enough of the new to provide for some change, yet enough of the old to remain respectable.

The young German-trained economists therefore found a receptive audience on their return to America. Even their excesses, their aura of disrespectability, were overlooked as simply the ardour of youth. The prodigal sons were received with the benign scepticism of their elders. Unlike Germany, there was no *Methodenstreit* in America. Dunbar, the leader of the 'old guard', set out to compare the two schools in his address, 'The Reaction in Political Economy'. 'After all,' he said,

. . . the difference between the old school and the new is

essentially a difference of emphasis or of relative weight given to the historical side of the subject, and not a radical change of method in arriving at economic truths. . . . It must be recognized as a fact . . . that political economy, as pursued by the deductive method, has severely disappointed the hopes which formerly centered around it; and this not merely because of the extravagance of the hopes, but also by reasons of its own sterility in results.[27]

Untempered by heat, conflicts between the two schools progressively weakened, and in 1892 reconciliation was formally recognized with the unanimous election of Dunbar to the presidency of the formerly 'historical' American Economic Association.

But perhaps the ultimate reason for the abrupt rise and fall of the American historical school was indicated by Frank Fetter. In reflecting on this 'remarkable chapter in economic theory', he recalled a phrase from Robert Louis Stevenson: 'It is as natural and right for a young man to be improvident and exaggerated as it is for old men to turn grey.'[28]

This would be the end of the story of the American historical school except for the tenacity of its leading advocate, Richard T. Ely, and his student, John R. Commons. Neither was antagonistic to the mainstream in economics, but both, largely out of personal taste, pursued courses of study indistinguishable from the programme of the historical school. Through Ely, Commons and their students, the historical tradition lives on in a limited degree in America – mainly at the University of Wisconsin. But under their auspices the doctrinal challenge of *Historismus* was forgotten. It became a subject-matter complementary to, rather than competitive with, the development of theoretical economics. As such it has persistently exercised a mildly beneficial influence in the development of American economics.

The importance of the historical school lies not in its real but rather in its imputed influence. When Veblen published his attack on mainstream economics, its defenders were barely over the *Methodenstreit*. It seemed to them that their recently defeated foe had found a new and even more powerful champion and was again on the rise. Worse, this Veblen seemed to be advocating an even more pernicious doctrine than the specfic *Historismus* in economics. It sounded like Hegel and the philosophy of history.

This in turn, added fuel to the still hot battle over Marxism. The old artillery from these wars was now trained against the institutionalists, and Veblen and Mitchell were caught up in the cross-fire. Ironically, Commons – who represented the wing most subject to criticism on these grounds – was hardly involved. Mitchell, as will be shown, made a few careless remarks which exposed him, but the case of Veblen was most piquant. Veblen had utter contempt both for the historical school of economics and for the philosophy of history. Indeed, he was one of their most formidable critics. Yet the conjuncture of his writings with these controversies caused him to be indelibly identified with both.

Eric Roll's confusion has already been mentioned in the previous chapter. Frank H. Knight attained an apogee by accusing Veblen of holding a doctrine that he, Knight, thought had never been better criticized than in a statement of Veblen's! First, he said, 'The truth about history and culture could hardly be better stated than it has been (paradoxical to observe) by the father of the new *Historismus* in American economics, Dr Thorstein Veblen ... "There are no cultural laws of the kind aimed at beyond the unprecise generalities that are sufficiently familiar beforehand to all passably intelligent adults." ' But Knight went on to say that Veblen himself holds the theory he has just so beautifully refuted, and that therefore he (Knight) need not waste his 'white paper' in refuting Veblen, in effect, with Veblen's own refutation.[29] To this one might readily assent.

In 1932 Lionel (now Lord) Robbins said, 'The only difference between Institutionalism and *Historismus* is that *Historismus* is much more interesting.'[30]

The result of this understandable misidentification of institutionalism with *Historismus* is that while institutionalists have received a great deal of criticism, it has never hit the mark. Confused and angered by accusations of what they do not believe, institutionalists have come to the conclusion that 'nobody understands us', and in a way they are right. But this has had a very detrimental effect on the development of institutionalism itself. Institutionalists have tended to withdraw from the arena of public debate and have enclosed themselves in a tight little circle of devotees. They have become inbred and careless. They seem to have lost the strong impetus to rigour, exactness and scholarship evinced by Veblen, Mitchell and Commons. It is as though the institutionalists have given up talking to anyone else, since no one understands them anyway, and have adopted a kind of semi-religious argot suitable only for communication among themselves. Perhaps the epitome of this tradition is Clarence E. Ayres, the most influential contemporary institutionalist, who, as is shown in Chapter 6, is nearly unquotable.

If the genuine merit of institutionalism is ever to be appreciated, it must first go through a critical purge. It must be forced out into the open and be subjected to the same standards of scholarship as other schools in economics. The first step in this process is to acknowledge that the identification between institutionalism and *Historismus* was an understandable, but basically erroneous, conception.[31] Only Ludwig von Mises, himself a major figure in the *Methodenstreit* and a leading critic of Marx, seemed able to discern the difference between institutionalism and these other heresies:

> The real issue was the epistemological foundations of the science of human action and its logical legitimacy. [Institution-alism was] positivism [that] recommended the substitution of an illusory social science which should adopt the logical structure and pattern of Newtonian mechanics.[32]

3 Thorstein Veblen

There are a number of lives of Veblen published by people of various degrees of skill and authority. The definitive work is Joseph Dorfman's encyclopedic *Thorstein Veblen and his America*. Wesley C. Mitchell wrote a most penetrating interpretative essay on Veblen as the editor's introduction to *What Veblen Taught*.[1] David Riesman[2] has written a bizarre 'interpretation' of Veblen in which Veblen's intellectual struggles are reduced to, and resolved by, psychological conflicts over father fixations and the like, drawing upon such 'data' as post-mortem studies of Veblen's first wife's sexual anatomy. Between these extremes lies a quantity of essays, reviews, obituaries and rumours readily accessible to the student of Veblenia and exhaustively compiled in Dorfman's book. The present discussion may thus be content with the bare biographical skeleton of his history[3] together with a few marginal notes on the highly personalized results of his life's work.

One of the more perplexing aspects of Veblen's work was the exceedingly playful frame of mind he brought to the pursuit of truth. He was not above pulling his reader's leg, and his 'desperately accurate circumlocutions, his perfectly elephantine means of expressing a platitude'[4] taxes both the language and the limit of his reader's endurance. Instead of painstaking efforts to describe the situation as accurately as the language permits, Veblen was content to under- or over-draw the portrait, with an often neglected admonition to the reader to make the 'suitable discount for error'; or to remind the reader that a given assertion may not be 'the truth, the whole truth, and nothing but the truth', but that 'it is true enough', or, at least, 'truer than the converse'. His references may vary from a broadside recommendation to the whole of Scandinavian archaeology, ethnology and mythology – including 'the backrooms of the museums' – to the mysterious 'they' in 'at least so they say'. And when he is obscure, it is, as

Lewis Mumford notes, 'not the result of accident' but the 'summit of a delicate effort'.[5]

But the reader often emerges from a limpid, lukewarm bath of delicately wrought obscurities and baroque circumlocutions, into a cutting gale of arctic invective. The household economy is portrayed as an experiment in 'conspicuous waste'; business men are discussed as 'saboteurs'; the kindly ecclesiastic is depicted as occupying 'the accredited vent for the exudation of effete material from the social organism'.[6]

The publication of *The Theory of the Leisure Class* created a social furore. 'Veblen girls' appeared; college boys spoke 'Veblenese'. People carefully forearmed themselves with an arsenal of Veblenian phrases before going to cocktail parties. Even H. L. Mencken felt a tremor in his comfortable lair as lion of society intellectuals. He became the 'God of the radicals whom he despised', and people read his book to, as he put it, 'giggle'.[7] A few years after publication of this book, someone asked Veblen if he was the author of *The Theory of the Leisure Class*. He replied, 'If I am, it has been a long time ago and I promise never to do it again.'[8]

Max Lerner believed this reception permanently affected Veblen's work: 'It was the intellectual isolation within which he had to work. He had disciples, he had students, he had detractors. But he had no genuine critics who would approach him with sympathy but who would insist on severe give and take.'[9]

But one can hardly blame potential critics. John Cummings was one of the few in print, and he lived to regret it. For example, Cummings was unfortunate enough to criticize Veblen's implication that much of language serves the purposes of invidious display. Veblen countered by noting that, of course, language serves not only this purpose but is also quite often used for purposes of communication. Having lured his prey, Veblen proceeded to slam the trap. 'This resort to the excluded middle,' he says, 'is in touch with the rhyme of a modern poet, who sings:

> I'd rather have fingers than toes;
> I'd rather have ears than a nose: etc.

overlooking the possibility of combining these several features in a single organism.'[10] Is it any wonder that Veblen 'had no genuine critics' after they witnessed the crucifixion of Mr Cummings, with all due pageant and circumstance, before their eyes? How one wishes Veblen could be reincarnated to write a review of David Riesman's 'interpretation'!

Some index of Veblen's despair over his intellectual isolation may be gleaned from this characterization of the state of economic science, as read to a meeting of the American Economic Association:

> If we are getting restless under the taxonomy of a monocotyle-donous wage doctrine and a cryptogramic theory of interest, with involute, loculicidial, tormentuous and moniliform variants, what is the cytoplasm, centrosome, or karyokinetic process to which we may turn and in which we may find sur-cease from the metaphysics of normality and controlling principles?[11]

Typically, Veblen was 'ill' when it was time to read this essay and the task devolved to a hapless substitute.

Rather than interpret Veblen's eccentricities as a result of his treatment by others, it is perhaps more accurate to describe Veblen as a man congenitally unable to appreciate the good opinion of others. While a more congenial man may have profited more from the community of science, or while a less fiercely individualistic personality may have turned out a more precise body of theory, he would not have been that curious mixture of genius and spleen that is Veblen, and that is a price one could not pay.

Thorstein Bunde Veblen was born on 30 July 1857, on a small farm in the Wisconsin frontier. His parents, Thomas and Kari Veblen, were Norwegian immigrants farming in this then frontier land. They preserved the customs and manners of the old country in the frontier isolation of their community, and Veblen grew up as a Norwegian. His father was a strong, taciturn man, endowed with a sceptical and penetrating mind. In the later years of his youth, Thorstein discussed social and philosophic questions with his father. These conversations were often carried far into the night under the protection of a great log fire in the rustic frontier cabin. Veblen later said of his father that 'he had never met a man his intellectual equal'.[12] His mother, on the other hand,

> ... was a high-spirited individual, warmly and electrically religious. Like a sturdy dominant woman of the sagas, she was

counsellor, adviser and often physician and surgeon in the community. . . . Thomas Veblen might take days, weeks, often years, in arriving at an answer to a problem, but Kari, with a 'brain that was the fastest machine God ever made' solved it 'in a fraction of a second'.[13]

In 1865, when Veblen was eight, the family moved still further into the frontier to Wheeling Township in Minnesota. This new community was even more intensely Norwegian than Wisconsin – it was actually a 'little Norway' transplanted to the plains of the Midwest. Few of the settlers (including Veblen's father) could speak English, and they vigorously fought any attempt by the public schools to teach it to their offspring. The community jealously preserved its Lutheran religion and the ancient lores and folkways of Norway against any foreign intrusion. Consequently,

Second generation children like Thorstein Veblen did not learn much of the alien tongue while in the settlement and were not touched by the alien culture. 'With the best that America might have offered to them they had no contact. It was entirely unknown to them.'[14]

The cultural isolationism of the community was sharply tempered by unscrupulous merchants and land speculators of the early American West. In Veblen's words:

This business was prevailingly of a prehensile character, being carried on by men well at home in the common law of the land and directed at getting something for nothing at the expense of the foreign immigrants who were unfamiliar with the common law. Being, in the view of their masters, aliens in the land, the foreign immigrants were felt to have no claim to consideration beyond what the laws that they did not know would formally secure to them in case matters were brought to the legal test. The presumption in the mind of honest businessmen at all points was on the side of their own pecuniary advantage, leaving any doubts to be settled by eventual litigation that might be brought by the foreign immigrants – who could with great uniformity be relied on most meticulously to avoid all litigation under a system of law with which they had no acquaintance, before local magistrates (businessmen) whom they had no reason to trust, in a language which they did not understand.[15]

Thus, Veblen spent his formative years in a community rigorously adhering to the old-world culture and whose main contact with the indigenous society was of a thoroughly negative character.

Veblen soon acquired a wide reputation in this little community as the nastiest boy around: '. . . he fought and bullied the boys, teased the girls, pestered the old people with stinging sarcasm and nicknames of such originality that they stuck through all the years'.[16]

Later, when he returned from college, his irreverent nature was veneered with a certain degree of sophistication – he now wrote these nicknames on his neighbours' fences in Greek! At a time when the Sioux were still scalping Norwegian settlers, and when many of the sons of Norway had lost their lives in the cause of the North in the Civil War, Veblen defended the Indians and the Confederates in local debates.

However much the community disliked this 'queer' boy, they admired his obvious intelligence:

At confirmation he proved more than a match for the examiner on the hair-splitting Lutheran church history and doctrine. He was expert in settling the never-ceasing disputes over the meaning of Norse terms which agitated the immigrants from the various rural sections of Norway, with their different dialects.[17]

In 1874 Veblen was called from the fields where he was working and put in a carriage, with his sister Emily. When he arrived at nearby Carleton College Academy, Thorstein Veblen knew that his father had decided to send him to college. Veblen did not get on well at Carleton. The Veblen children could only remain in school by exercising the utmost economy. They dressed in homemade clothes made by their mother and lived in a small house their father built on a lot adjoining the college campus. These obvious signs of poverty and their natural rusticity set them off as a class apart from the proper Yankee tradition of Carleton. Although Thorstein and Andrew, his brother, each won the 'Atkins Prize' of $80 for the best entrance examinations, they felt that many of the prizes and honours normally due to them were withheld. Thorstein was more sensitive to these petty provocations than was Andrew and, not content simply to endure them, he replied in kind.

Consequently the students at Carleton thought he was 'sneering and supercilious' while most of the faculty 'was not enthusiastic over this youth with a "mind clothed in sardonic humor"'.[18] His only friend on the faculty was J. B. Clarke — a self-described 'Professor of Odds and Ends' at Carleton. Clark (who was to become one of the greatest economists in America) admired Veblen's obvious abilities and was immensely pleased when Veblen became famous in later life, although some of this fame was at Clark's own expense. Veblen's effect upon the serene life at Carleton is shown in the following account:

The weekly public declamation exercises, or rhetoricals, presided over by the professor of philosophy, provided Veblen with his best opportunity for jarring the faculty and students. While Carleton prayed for the conversion of the heathen, Veblen, reader of Swift, delivered 'A Plea for Cannibalism' which threw the faculty and students into an uproar. On another occasion he delivered 'An Apology for a Toper'. According to the prevailing morals, drunkenness would and should bring severe retribution, but Veblen noted how drunkards actually viewed death, not how they should view it, and closed with the statement that 'although death is never far away, it has for them few terrors'. Clarke who was presiding, asked him if he was apologizing for the toper, but Veblen casually replied that he was simply engaged in a scientific observation. At other times he astonished the gathering with oratorical outbursts on 'The Science of Laughter', 'The Face of a Worn-Out Politician', 'The Absence of the Gregarious in Student Life', 'Companions That Can Be Counted On', 'Thrice is he Armed that Hathe his Quarrel Just', 'Two Ways of Looking at Facts'.

. . .

At one meeting, the official critic called attention to the brevity and poor quality of the papers, declaring that they had little depth and showed little thought in preparation. Veblen appeared at the next meeting with a paper on the philosophy of Mill. For over forty minutes he read it, page after page, very seriously and in a dreary monotone. Without understanding a word the listeners gave it the best attention they could —

expecting each moment that he would come to a close. When it was finally finished, the critic was forced to admit that 'Mr Veblen's paper was sufficiently long and sufficiently deep'.[19]

Veblen ended his career at Carleton by taking the junior and senior years at once. His graduation oration on 'Mill's Examination of Hamilton's Philosophy of the Conditioned' was received in the local newspaper report with an admixture of admiration, awe and wonder: 'Veblen, son of Thor, in spite of the heat, hammered away blow upon blow, and with no mean skill, at a subject the bare name of which was almost an overdose for the average reader.'[20]

After graduation from Carleton, Veblen taught for one year in a small academy in Madison, Wisconsin. When the academy closed, Veblen decided to accompany his brother to the newly-formed graduate school of Johns Hopkins. There he studied under Richard T. Ely and the philosopher Charles H. Pierce. Ely influenced him very little, Pierce, perhaps some. [21] These contacts did not last long, however, for he soon left to study philosophy under President Noah Porter at Yale.

Veblen arrived at Yale in the midst of the great 'evolutionist' controversy between Porter and William Graham Sumner. Sumner, a disciple of Herbert Spencer, wanted to use Spencer's *Study of Sociology* as a text. Porter disapproved and eventually forbade it. The ensuing battle between these two very determined men rocked Yale to its foundations and divided both students and faculty into bitterly opposed camps. Sumner's final triumph changed the curriculum of Yale and later of virtually all American universities away from the divinity school atmosphere which had prevailed.

Strangely enough, Veblen, who was distinguished both then and in his later years by the ability to start controversy where none existed before, was the friend of both sides, admired and respected by each camp. He became known as 'Porter's chum' because of the long walks they took together, discussing philosophical questions. Sumner attempted to get Veblen to expand his prize-winning ($250) essay on the disposal of the impending government surplus of funds into a doctoral dissertation in economics, but Veblen was still primarily interested in philosophy.[22] He utilized these years at Yale to make extensive inquiries into the

writings of Hegel, Spencer and Kant, and his paper on the latter's
then untranslated *Critique of Judgment* was published in the
Journal of Speculative Philosophy in 1884. In this same year he
finished his dissertation, 'Ethical grounds of a Doctrine of Retribution' (which has never been found), and obtained the Ph.D.

The seven years of Veblen's life after graduation were years of
frustration. In spite of the revolution that was gradually sweeping
over America's institutions of higher learning, this ill-mannered,
poorly dressed, uncouth 'Norskie', suspected of agnostic leanings,
could not obtain a university post for all his admitted brilliance.
Veblen spent these dismal years on his father's farm in Minnesota
and, after he married Ellen Role in 1888, on her father's farm at
Stacyville, Iowa. He read voraciously during these years, 'novels,
poetry, hymnbooks as well as learned treatises. As one pile of books
disappeared, he promptly secured another.'[23] One of these books
was Edward Bellamy's *Looking Backward*, which Veblen and his
wife read aloud. '. . . I believe that this was the turning-point in
our lives,' Ellen wrote, curiously, 'because it so affected me.' She
thought her emphasis on this aspect of her husband's interests may
have helped to turn the balance at that 'critical period before his
life work began'.[24] Certainly, Veblen's development of the themes
of 'conspicuous consumption', of the conflict of interest between
the businessman and the community, and his examination of the
disutility of labour, bear a close resemblance to Bellamy's earlier,
brilliant work.[25]

In 1891 Veblen determined to end his enforced absence from
the academic world by any means possible. With his family's
financial aid, he once again set off for the university, this time as a
'graduate student' at Cornell. There Veblen met J. Laurence
Laughlin – one of the leading classical economists of the time.

> Laughlin often told the story of his first meeting with Veblen.
> He was sitting in his study in Ithaca when an anaemic-looking
> person, wearing a coonskin cap and corduroy trousers, entered,
> and in the mildest possible tone announced – 'I am Thorstein
> Veblen.'[26]

The ensuing conversation so impressed Laughlin that he obtained
a fellowship for Veblen although all the normal fellowships were
already filled. When Laughlin went to the newly-formed University of Chicago, he took Veblen with him as a fellow. Veblen

taught a few classes there and became the *de facto* editor of the *Journal of Political Economy*. In spite of his very valuable services for the *Journal* as editor, reviewer and contributor, Veblen was able to remain at the university only through Laughlin's personal influence with the administration. He was an exceptionally poor pedagogue, and he did not 'advertise the university'. Consequently, Veblen, at the age of forty-two, was still only an instructor at the University of Chicago!

Then, in 1899, Veblen published *The Theory of the Leisure Class*. The name of this obscure instructor shot to international fame. He had now sufficiently 'advertised the university' and was accordingly made assistant professor (1900). Veblen, however, realized the precariousness of his position in the university and began casting about for another job. He found that the position of chief of the Division of Documents in the Library of Congress was open and applied there. This application reveals the prodigious command of languages he had acquired by then – 'German, French, Spanish, Italian, Dutch and the Scandinavian languages including Icelandic' – and some view of Veblen in the eyes of his contemporaries through the recommendations sent by various people. J. B. Clark wrote, 'Keen analytical power is his marked characteristic but he unites with this trait a phenomenal capacity and inclination for work. . . .'[27] Davenport said, 'I regard Veblen as without a rival in this country in those lines of economic thought lying nearest to Philosophy, (that is) in the History of Economic Thought, in the History of Economic Institutions, and in the Literature and History of Socialism.'[28] Mitchell said, 'If ability as a student of social questions is of weight in determining the selection of a man for the post, I do not think there is another man in the country who has qualifications equal to those of Mr Veblen.'[29]

Illustrative of the non-partisan spirit in which Veblen approached his solicitations, he requested one from a certain 'Jenks', who 'thought Veblen was all bluff'.[30]

One might also mention, in this connection, his recommendations at another time regarding an archaeological expedition to Crete he wished to organize under the auspices of the Carnegie Foundation. Allyn A. Young wrote, 'Veblen is the most gifted man I have known.'[31] Taussig said, 'A brother economist, in whose judgment I have much confidence, once remarked to me in con-

versation that Veblen came as near to being a genius as any economist we have; and I am inclined to think that the remark was
just.'[32]

Veblen obtained neither position.

At about this time of Veblen's application to the Library of
Congress, President David Starr Jordan of Stanford was com-
bating a 'vocational school' movement instigated by his trustees.
He hired Veblen in order to put more weight on his side of the
battle. As Jordan said, 'What he cannot reverse and make appear
the opposite of what it purports to be isn't worth reversing.'[33]
Veblen went to Stanford in 1906 and stayed there three years,
finally driven out by scandal. As Veblen wrote to a friend, 'The
president doesn't approve of my domestic arrangements. Nor do
I.'[34]

Davenport, Veblen's former student, was now head of the
Department of Economics at the University of Missouri, and he
persuaded President Hill to employ Veblen there. Veblen spent
the first part of his stay in Columbia in a tent erected in Davenport's basement, entering and exiting through a nearby basement
window. In spite of this, however, he did not enjoy his stay:

> The local Chamber of Commerce offered a prize for a slogan
> for the town, and Veblen told Walter Stewart, a student and
> colleague, that it ought to be described as a 'wood-pecker hole
> of a town . . .' to which he later added, '. . . in a rotten stump
> called Missouri'.[35]

Veblen stayed on at Missouri for seven years, after which he
worked for a short time during the First World War for the
United States Food Administration and, in 1918, on the editorial
board of *The Dial* magazine.

In 1919 Veblen became a member of the staff of the New
School for Social Research in New York. He, Wesley C. Mitchell,
Charles A. Beard and James Harvey Robinson were the 'big
four' on this staff. John Dewey, who kept his Columbia professor-
ship, Harold J. Laski, Harry Elmer Barnes, Graham Wallas and
Dean Roscoe Pound were also in this faculty. This brilliant early
promise, however, was not realized, and in 1922 the 'New School'
had to cull its staff. Veblen set out once more looking for a job.

He never found one; these last seven years of his life were lonely,
frustrating years. He applied to Clark University and to a

Scandinavian university for a position but never obtained one. He wrote *Absentee Ownership*, his last book, published a few more articles and his thirty-seven-year-old translation of the *Laxdaela Saga*. Veblen died on 3 August 1929:

> It is also my wish, in case of death, to be cremated, if it can conveniently be done, as expeditiously and inexpensively as may be, without ritual or ceremony of any kind; that my ashes be thrown into the sea; or into some sizeable stream running into the sea; that no tombstone, slab, epitaph, effigy, tablet, inscription or monument of any name or nature be set up in my memory or name in any place or at any time; that no obituary, memorial, portrait or biography of me, nor any letters written to or by me be printed or re-published, or in any way reproduced, copied or circulated.[36]

Joseph Dorfman includes at the end of his biography of Veblen a complete bibliography of Veblen's work. In looking this bibliography over, one cannot but be struck by the constancy of Veblen's thought through the many years his works encompass. As Mitchell says, 'His works are so much of one piece that almost any one of his disquisitions serves as an introduction to the whole.'[37] His early essays are exploratory preludes to his books; his later essays are mostly extensions of his books. This is uniformly true up to the outbreak of the Great War when, gradually, but increasingly, Veblen allowed himself to be drawn away from his theoretical interests to questions of the hour, to prognostications of the future. Veblen's work suffered as these questions came to occupy his attention. His later works lose much of the brilliance and studious craftsmanship of his earlier efforts. More importantly his progressive concern with the problems of the moment deflected his attention away from the development of his theory.

Thus, his *Absentee Ownership* may profitably have stuck to the strict theoretical structure of the earlier *Theory of Business Enterprise* and developed in greater detail the theory of money, credit and interest in the earlier work. *The Vested Interests and the Common Man* could usefully have been sacrificed in order to revise, extend and clear up the lacunae in his *Instinct of Workmanship*. Veblen was fully aware of the limitations of his early works, and it is unfortunate that he did not return to them.

Veblen's first major work was his Ph.D. dissertation at Yale, 'The Ethical Grounds of a Theory of Retribution' (lost). His first published work, 'Kant's Critique of Judgment' in the *Journal of Speculative Philosophy* in 1884, testifies to his early competence in the field of philosophy and influenced the course of his later work.

In 1891 Veblen began the period of his greatest productivity, with the publication of 'Some Neglected Points in the Theory of Socialism'. In this essay are found the preliminary ideas of his *Theory of the Leisure Class*. It is not too much to say that the 1890s witnessed the development of all the essentials of Veblen's thought. In 1892 the groundwork of his second major work, *The Theory of Business Enterprise*, was laid with the two essays, 'Böhm-Bawerk's Definition of Capital and the Theory of Wages' and, especially, with 'The Overproduction Fallacy'. 1894 witnessed the amusing 'Economic Theory of Women's Dress', 1895 his translation of Gustav Cohen's *System der Finanzwissenschaft*. In 1898–1900 he advanced his frontal assault on received economic theory with the great charges, 'Why is Economics not an Evolutionary Science?' and 'The Preconceptions of Economic Science'. 1899 also marks the publication of his first and most popular book, *The Theory of the Leisure Class*, and his first and only reply to a critic – the masterful and scathing 'Mr Cummings' Strictures on *The Theory of the Leisure Class*'.

The next decade and a half, up to the outbreak of the First World War, marks the period of what might be called the 'consolidation' of his theory. In 1900 he published 'Industrial and Pecuniary Employments' – the groundwork of his economic theory – and in 1901, 'Gustav Schmoller's Economics', which may be viewed as Veblen's attempt to settle in his own mind his position vis-à-vis the German historical school. This position was appreciative but essentially negative. In 1904 *The Theory of Business Enterprise* – his 'economic' theory – appeared[38] and in 1905 an important amendment to this book, 'Credit and Prices'. In 1906 he published 'The Place of Science in Modern Civilization'. This article provides a major turning-point in Veblen's work and with it his basic social theory was completed. He then turned his attention to competing theories with 'Professor Clark's Economics' and the 'Economics of Karl Marx and his Followers' (both 1906). The latter surely deserves a place among the classics of

Marxist criticism. From 1906 to 1914 Veblen continued his critical examination of other theories with respect to his own: thus, 'Fisher's Capital and Income' (1907); 'On the Nature of Capital' (1908); 'Fisher's Rate of Interest' and 'The Limitations of Marginal Utility' (1909). It is interesting to note, by the way, that Fisher replied to Veblen's strictures. Veblen, Fisher said, dismissed virtually all of what he attempted to do and concentrated on the methodological implications of his work, whereas he (Fisher) agreed with Veblen's methodological strictures and thought Veblen made only a 'mistake in taxonomy' by placing himself (Fisher) 'on his *index expurgatorius*'.[39]

In 1914 Veblen published what seemed to him his most important book,[40] *The Instinct of Workmanship and the State of the Industrial Arts*. This book and the war of the same year mark another turning-point in Veblen's work. With the possible exception of *Imperial Germany and the Industrial Revolution* (1915) and *An Inquiry into the Nature of Peace and the Terms of its Perpetuation* (1917), Veblen was never again to reach the heights of his earlier work. These last two books, though they contain many interesting digressions into new fields, are mainly concerned with the policy implications of his basic theory – at the expense of the development of this theory itself. His writings after 1914 are almost exclusively occupied with the specific questions of war or of the impending depression he foresaw.

In 1915 he published the 'Opportunity of Japan' in which he prophetically contended that the only thing that kept Japan from joining the war on the side of Germany was the uncertainty of success. In 1918 came 'On the General Principles of a Policy of Reconstruction', and his eloquent plea for America to open her doors to the dispossessed intellectuals of Europe, 'The War and the Higher Learning'. He also published *The Higher Learning in America: A Memorandum on the Conduct of Universities by Businessmen* – a savagely biting satire on American universities. In 1919 *The Vested Interests and the Common Man* – an indifferent work; and his last flicker of brilliance as an essayist, the very stimulating and profound 'The Intellectual Pre-eminence of the Jews in Modern Europe'.

In 1920 he reviewed Keynes' *Economic Consequences of the Peace* and provided the much-needed political and sociological background to that great work. In 1921, *The Engineers and the*

Price System – a very poor, very strained parody of his own theory – where he toyed with the idea of a government by engineers whose 'matter-of-fact' mentality, due to their intimate association with the 'machine process', should make them desirable leaders. Ironically, but perhaps also characteristically, this book had the most measurable success and influence. It formed the theoretical basis of the brief but influential movement of 'technocracy' in the early years of the depression in the United States.

In 1923 he published *Absentee Ownership and Business Enterprise in Recent Times: The Case of America*, wherein he utterly missed the chance to revise his basic social theory and to incorporate into it his specifically economic contributions. In 1925 he delivered his parting blast at the economic profession with 'Economic Theory in the Calculable Future'. In 1927 he wrote 'An Experiment in Eugenics' (first published in *Essays in our Changing Order*), which has the distinction only of being his last published piece.

In addition to the works by Dorfman, Mitchell and Riesman already mentioned, there have been innumerable dissertations and several other publications on Veblen and/or the institutionalists. The first was *The Trend of Economics* (1930), 'the manifesto of the younger generation of American economists', with essays by Rexford G. Tugwell (ed.), M. A. Copeland, Wesley C. Mitchell, Frank H. Knight and others.

Perhaps the most critical book yet published on Veblen was Richard Victor Teggert's *Thorstein Veblen: A Chapter in American Economic Thought* (1932). Teggert's unsympathetic view led him to miss the best of Veblen but make some very telling criticisms of the worst.

In 1937 J. A. Hobson published *Veblen*, a very searching yet sympathetic critique of Veblen's social theory. Hobson was the first to detect the strong behaviouristic strain in Veblen's theory and to take him to task for it. In addition he felt Veblen's attack on mainstream economics was overdone.

Certainly the best work on Veblen's philosophy to date is Stanley Matthew Daugert's *The Philosophy of Thorstein Veblen* (1950). If Daugert can be faulted, it is only because the 'two Veblens', mentioned before, were too elusive for him to track down. Nevertheless Daugert had a profound insight into Veblen's philosophy and the present study is much indebted to this earlier work.

In 1948 Louis Scheider published a book on the very interesting subject, *The Freudian Psychology and Veblen's Social Theory*. One can hardly blame Scheider for not being able adequately to relate the two most difficult thinkers in social philosophy.

There are several books concerned with summaries and applications of Veblen and institutionalist theories. Since these works are, for the most part, not within the specific purview of the present study, they may be listed without comment:

John S. Gambs, *Beyond Supply and Demand: A Reappraisal of Institutional Economics* (1946);
H. M. Kelly, *Contemporary Economic Thought: The Contribution of Neo-Institutional Economics* (1972);
Douglas F. Dowd, *Thorstein Veblen* (1966);
Jay M. Gould, *The Technical Elite* (1966).

There have been several magazine articles on Veblen. Two of the more notable were the very sympathetic review of Veblen in *Fortune* (December 1947) – complete with a picture of an amusing oil painting of Veblen (now hanging at Yale University) – and the double issue on Veblen by the socialist magazine, the *Monthly* Review (July–August) 1957). Its editor, Paul M. Sweezy, concluded that while there were differences, at heart he was one of us.

There is also the disappointing *Veblen: A play in Three Acts* by Leonard S. Silk (1966).

In 1963 the Institute of Industrial Relations of the University of California (Los Angeles) sponsored a series of lectures on 'Institutional Economics: Veblen, Commons and Mitchell Reconsidered'. In celebration of the centenary of Carleton College, a series of lectures was held (and published in 1968 under the editorship of Carleton C. Qualey) in honour of 'the college's celebrated and most significant alumnus' – 'Thorstein Veblen (Class of 1880)'.

4 Selected Veblenia

This chapter presents a small sampling of Veblen's writings on subjects as diverse as Karl Marx, dogs and cats, women's dress, and the intellectual qualities of Jews. Veblen touched on nearly everything in his writings and nearly everything he touched was transmogrified into the opposite of what it appeared to be. This is a very small sample which could be extended almost indefinitely. That is left to the reader. These selections are offered only as bait to those not already hooked on Veblen.

I. THE 'EMULATION COMPLEX'[1]

'Emulation' indicates a drive to equal or excel one's fellows in whatever terms they specify. Although it would be too much to contend that emulation was not recognized as a powerful element in social relations before Veblen's work, it is fair to say that he, more than any other, explicated it and developed its implications into a theory of human behaviour. In this sense, Veblen can fairly claim to have discovered emulation as a scientific concept. It is certainly one of his greatest contributions to social science.

Although the 'emulation complex' is most closely associated with Veblen's *Theory of the Leisure Class*, where it was employed in a satirical vein, perhaps the best concise statement appeared seven years before in an article entitled 'Some Neglected Points in the Theory of Socialism'. Some space is devoted to an exposition of the emulation complex in both accounts not only because of its intrinsic importance to social theory, but also because in these discussions the many inventive, satirical, playful yet rigorous facets of Veblen's mind are brought into full play.

The article on 'Some Neglected Points in the Theory of Socialism' was written in response to a thesis advanced by Herbert Spencer in an article entitled 'From Freedom to Bondage'. Spencer's thesis was, briefly, that the revolutionary programmes of socialism were basically unsound. He particularly rejected the idea that 'things are so bad that society must be pulled to pieces and reorganized on another plan'. On the contrary, Spencer pointed to the 'obvious improvements' in the condition of the average man under the capitalist regime. Spencer concluded, therefore, that the socialist programme was groundless, that (in Veblen's words) 'the popular unrest is due essentially to a feeling of ennui – to a desire for a change of posture on the part of the social body'.

Veblen's analysis consists in a search for a deeper cause of unrest, for if Spencer is wrong in his diagnosis, if on the contrary 'this popular sentiment is found to be the outgrowth of any of the essential features of the existing social system, the chances of its ultimately working a radical change in the system will be much greater'.

Veblen begins by conceding, even strengthening Spencer's major thesis:

> The ground of discontent cannot lie in a disadvantageous comparison of the present with the past, so far as material interests are concerned. It is notorious, and, practically, none of the agitators deny, that the system of industrial competition, based on private property, has brought about, or has at least co-existed with, the most rapid advance in average wealth and industrial efficiency that the world has seen. . . . The claim that the system of competition has proved itself an engine for making the rich richer and the poor poorer has the fascination of epigram; but if its meaning is that the lot of the average, of the masses of humanity is civilized life, is worse today, as measured in the means of livelihood, than it was twenty, or fifty, or a hundred years ago, then it is farcical.

However, he says,

> There is a sense in which the aphorism is true. . . . The existing system has not made, and does not tend to make, the industrious poor poorer as measured absolutely in means of livelihood; but it does tend to make them relatively poorer in their own eyes, as measured in terms of comparative economic importance, and, curious as it may seem at first sight, that is what seems to count. . . . There is a not inconsiderable amount of physical privation

suffered by many people in this country, which is not physically
necessary. The cause is very often that what might be the means
of comfort is diverted to the purpose of maintaining a decent
appearance, or even a show of luxury.

Thus, Veblen introduced his major theme – one of the 'neglected points':

Man as we find him today has much regard to his good fame –
to his standing in the esteem of his fellow-men. This characteristic he has always had, and no doubt will always have. . . .
Regard for one's reputation means, in the average of cases,
emulation. It is a striving to be, and more immediately to be
thought to be, better than one's neighbors.

Veblen notes that at various times and places the criteria under
which one is appraised by one's fellow-men and, hence, the criteria under which one appraises oneself, vary. Piety, predatory
exploits, birth, scholarship and even virtue, all have had their time
and place. But the modern regime

is pre-eminently an industrial, economic society, and it is industrial – economic – excellence that most readily attracts the
approving regard of that society. . . . When we say that a man
is 'worth' so many dollars, the expression does not convey the
idea that moral or other personal excellence is to be measured
in terms of money, but it does very distinctly convey the idea
that the fact of his possessing many dollars is very much to his
credit.

He then introduces 'a further, secondary stage' of economic
emulation which was later to become 'conspicuous consumption':

One does not 'make much of a showing' in the eyes of the large
majority of the people whom one meets with, except by an
unremitting demonstration of ability to pay. That is practically
the only means which the average of us have of impressing our
respectability on the many to whom we are personally
unknown, but whose transient good opinion we would so gladly
enjoy. So it comes about that the appearance of success is very
much to be desired, and is even in many cases preferred to the
substance. We all know how nearly indispensable it is to afford

whatever expenditures other people with whom we class our-
selves can afford, and also that it is desirable to afford a little
something more than others.

The consequence is

that this emulation in expenditure stands ever ready to absorb
any margin of income that remains after ordinary physical
wants and comforts have been provided for, and, further, that
it presently becomes as hard to give up that part of one's
habitual 'standard of living' which is due to the struggle for
respectability, as it is to give up many physical comforts. In a
general way, the need of expenditure in this direction grows as
fast as the means of satisfying it, and, in the long run, a large
expenditure comes no nearer satisfying the desire than a smaller
one.

For example:

As we are all aware, the chief element of value in many articles
of apparel is not their efficiency for protecting the body, but for
protecting the wearer's respectability; and that not only in the
eyes of one's neighbors but even in one's own eyes. Indeed, it
happens not very rarely that a person chooses to go ill-clad in
order to be well dressed.

Now, to proceed to the question of socialist agitation:

. . . the easier the conditions of physical life for modern civilized
man become, and the wider the horizon of each and the extent
of the personal contact of each with his fellows, the greater will
lie the preponderance of economic success as a means of emulation, and the greater the straining after economic respectability.
Inasmuch as the aim of emulation is not any absolute degree
of comfort or of excellence, no advance in the average well-
being of the community can end the struggle or lessen the strain.
A general amelioration cannot quiet the unrest whose source is
the craving of everybody to compare favorably with his
neighbor.

.   .   .

Human nature being what it is, the struggle of each to possess
more than his neighbor is inseparable from the institution of

private property. And also, human nature being what it is, one
who possesses less will, on the average, be jealous of the one who
possesses more; and 'more' means not more than the average
share, but more than the share of the person who makes the
comparison.

Thus,

Under modern conditions the struggle for existence has, in a
very appreciable degree, been transformed into a struggle to
keep up appearances. The ground of unrest with which we
are concerned is, very largely, jealousy – envy, if you choose;
and the ground of this particular form of jealousy, that moves
for socialism, is to be found in the institution of private property.

So much for Spencer. Capitalism has diverted the emulative
propensity to material goods 'which no advance in the average
well-being of the community . . . can satisfy'. Thus, it has bred, if
not the seeds of its destruction as Marx would have it, at least the
seeds of socialist discontent.

Veblen then proceeds to another neglected point, one 'bearing
on the question of the practicability' of socialism:

Under a regime which should allow no inequality of acquisition
or of income, this form of emulation, which is due to the possibility of such inequality, would also tend to become obsolete.
With the abolition of private property, the characteristic of
human nature which now finds its exercise in this form of
emulation, should logically find exercise in other, perhaps
nobler and socially more serviceable activities. It is at any rate
not easy to imagine its running into any line of action more
futile or less worthy of human effort.

Veblen concludes with a quantitative estimate:

. . . I believe it is within the mark to suppose that the struggle
to keep up appearances is chargeable, directly and indirectly,
with one-half of the aggregate labor, and abstinence from labor
– for the standard of respectability requires us to shun labor as
well as to enjoy the fruits of it – on part of the American people.

It is accordingly competent for the advocates of the nationali-
zation of industry and property to claim that even if their
scheme of organization should prove less effective for production of goods than the present, as measured absolutely in terms
of the aggregate output of our industry, yet the community
might readily be maintained at the present average standard of
comfort.

Veblen concludes his discussion with an appraisal of the feasi-
bility of moving towards a socialist state on this basis. He indicates
that it might be worth trying, but there is the very real danger
that the socialist state would create its own 'regime of status, a
bureaucracy, which would be unendurable'. In this eventuality,
he indicates that the present system, with all its real if not apparent
inefficiency and discontent, would be preferable.

In *The Theory of the Leisure Class*,[2] Veblen follows the thin
red line of emulation through all its various manifestations of
'conspicuous consumption', 'pecuniary emulation', 'invidious
display', 'conspicuous leisure' and 'pecuniary canons of taste' in
contemporary culture. In this book he writes, as someone has
recently said of another author, 'as though he had a jeweler's lens
screwed into each eye'. The end-effect is rather like one of those
unique and appalling visions of the world normally seen only in
such graphic arts as Hieronymus Bosch's famous triptych, 'The
Garden of Delights'.

The keystone of contemporary culture, Veblen contends, is
simply ostentatious waste – of money, time, resources and effort.
Our notions of the true, the good and the beautiful are modelled
by the imperative of conspicuous waste, and accordingly, since
these notions are what makes life worth living, our lives are energetically devoted to that cause. The following is a small sampling
of Veblen's diagnosis of the role of the emulation complex and its
wasteful, predacious manifestations in everyday life.

Women

The socially accredited function of women, Veblen says, is (*a*) to
stand as a chattel property – a trophy of male powers; (*b*) to direct
the household in various forms of conspicuous consumption; and
(*c*) to provide evidence of vicarious leisure so as to uphold the good
name of the husband:

It is still felt that woman's life, in its civil, economic, and social bearing, is essentially and normally a vicarious life, the merit or demerit of which is, in the nature of things, to be imputed to some other individual who stands in some relation of ownership or tutelage to the woman.

.   .   .

The dress of women goes even farther than that of men in the way of demonstrating the wearer's abstinence from productive employment. . . . The substantial reason for our tenacious attachment to the skirt is just this: it is expensive and it hampers the wearer at every turn and incapacitates her for all useful exertion. . . . The corset is, in economic theory, substantially a mutilation, undergone for the purpose of lowering the subject's vitality and rendering her permanently and obviously unfit for work. It is true, the corset impairs the personal attractions of the wearer, but the loss suffered in that score is offset by the gain in reputability which comes of her visibly increased expensiveness and infirmity.

'Clothes' last too long to meet the requirements of conspicuous consumption; hence, 'style'. 'We readily, and for the most part with utter sincerity, find those things pleasing that are in vogue.' And 'The process of developing an aesthetic nausea takes more or less time; the length of time required in any given case being inversely as the degree of intrinsic odiousness of the style in question.'

Veblen approvingly noted the 'double watchword' of the 'New Woman' movement – 'Emancipation' and 'Work'. Perhaps that is why women found him irresistible!

Dogs and Cats

Dogs are better than cats in terms of conventional standards:

The dog has advantages in the way of uselessness as well as in special gifts of temperament. . . . He is the filthiest of the domestic animals in his person and the nastiest in his habits. For this, he makes up in a servile fawning attitude towards his master, and a readiness to inflict damage and discomfort on all else.

.   .   .

The cat is less reputable . . . because she is less wasteful. She may even serve a useful function. At the same time, the cat's temperament does not fit her for the honorific purpose. She lives with man on terms of equality. . . .

Domestic Flora

Flowers are similar in respect to 'Pecuniary beauty' . . . by habitually identifying beauty with reputability, it comes about, that a beautiful article which is not expensive is not accounted beautiful . . . some beautiful flowers pass conventionally for offensive weeds . . . [others] are rejected as vulgar by those people who are better able to pay for expensive flowers and who are educated to a higher schedule of pecuniary beauty in the florist's products; while still other flowers, of no greater intrinsic beauty than these, are cultivated at great cost and call out much admiration from flower-lovers whose tastes have been developed under the critical guidance of a polite environment.

Lawns and parks are an atavistic throwback to the pastoral stage of human history; as such they should properly be grazed by cows, but:

The vulgar suggestion of thrift, which is nearly inseparable from the cow, is a standing objection to the decorative use of this animal . . . the cow's place is often given to some more or less inadequate substitute, such as deer, antelope, or some such exotic beast. These substitutions . . . are . . . preferred because of their superior expensiveness or futility, and their consequent repute. They are not vulgarly lucrative either in fact or in suggestion.

Architecture

Impressive buildings, public and private, 'present an endless variety of architectural distress and suggestions of expensive discomfort. Considered as objects of beauty, the dead walls of the sides and back of these structures, left untouched by the hands of the artists, are commonly the best features of the building.'

Heaven

'. . . an extreme case [of celestial conspicuous consumption] occurs in the devout imagery of the Negro population of the South. Their word-painters are unable to descend to anything cheaper than gold; so that in this case the insistence on pecuniary beauty gives a startling effect in yellow – such as would be unbearable to a soberer taste.'

Sportsmanship and Make-believe

It is noticeable, for instance, that even mild-mannered and matter-of-fact men who go out shooting are apt to carry an excess of arms and accoutrements in order to impress upon their own imagination the seriousness of their undertaking. These huntsmen are also prone to a histrionic, prancing gait and to an elaborate exaggeration of the motions, whether of stealth or onslaught, involved in their deeds of exploit.

Each sport has its own locutions – usually 'sanguinary'. And 'the use of slang in any employment is probably to be accepted as evidence that the occupation in question is substantially make-believe.'

Veblen's theory of the emulation complex has been translated into the more familiar jargon of economics in terms of Veblen effects – demand depending on high price for status purposes – and the ratchet effect, where upward shifts in consumption levels are easier than downward shifts. The ratchet effect has been used as a counter-argument to the theory of secular stagnation, which contemplated a state wherein consumers would become satiated to the point that continued economic growth would be in jeopardy. Veblen's theory provides an avenue of escape from this (horrible) fate by showing that since demands are based on relative well-being in terms of status rather than absolute well-being in terms of comfort, the consumer can be relied upon to purchase as much as can conceivably be made. Few economists have questioned this ideal of limitless growth, but a few have. John Kenneth Galbraith, who resembles Veblen in wit, inventiveness and courage, has expressed some reservations in this regard. He notes that, in Veblen, 'One observes the struggle between hens for social pre-eminence in the chicken yard as an interesting phenomenon but in so doing, one does not do much to underwrite the social values of the birds.'[3] Kenneth Boulding is another such economist; as he correctly observes of Veblen, he was among the first to challenge the idea of the 'immaculate conception of the indifference curve'.[4]

But one is left with the nagging suspicion that Veblen's discovery of the emulation complex has not yet been fully exploited. Perhaps the reason is that there is not yet a general theory that can fully withstand its implications or digest its consequences. This is shown particularly in its conventional use in economic theory. The possibility of 'interdependent utility functions' is recognized, only to be immediately assumed out of the model because, with interdependence, the criterion of Pareto optimality begins to disintegrate. It is possible that everyone can be worse off with more goods. Veblen's discovery of emulation sets up an insistent demand for a sensible theory of value in economics. It demands a means of sorting 'goods' from 'bads' in terms of personal values and social ethics. That is too much for modern 'positive' social science to stomach.

2. 'THE SOCIALIST ECONOMICS OF KARL MARX AND HIS FOLLOWERS'[5]

Except as a whole and except in light of its postulates and aims, the Marxian system is not only not tenable, but it is not even intelligible. A discussion of a given isolated feature of the system (such as the theory of value) from the point of view of classical economics (such as that offered by Böhm-Bawerk) is as futile as a discussion of solids in terms of two dimensions.

With this drum roll, Veblen opens a three-pronged attack on Marx, his followers, and on the critics of Marx. He counters the attack from the Right by attempting to show that they have fundamentally misunderstood the premises and aims of the Marxian system. Then he vanquishes the Left by demonstrating that, once properly understood, the Marxian system is quite primitive from an evolutionary, scientific point of view. After putting to rout the major forces of the Marxian Left and the Austrian Right, he circumspectly mops up the scattered bands of 'followers' spread in a disarray over the battlefield. Whatever its ultimate validity, Veblen's attack on Karl Marx, his followers and his critics represents an astonishing intellectual *tour de force*:

As regards these preconceptions and postulates, Marx draws on two distinct lines of antecedents – the Materialistic Hegelianism and the English system of Natural Rights. By his earlier training he is an adept in the Hegelian method of speculation and inoculated with the metaphysics of development underlying the Hegelian system. By his later training he is an expert in the system of Natural Rights and Natural Liberty, ingrained in his ideals of life and held inviolate throughout.... The ideals of his propaganda are natural-rights ideals, but his theory of the working out of these ideals in the course of history rests on the Hegelian metaphysics of development, and his method of speculation and construction of theory is given by the Hegelian dialectic.

Marx belongs to the 'materialistic' wing of Hegelianism which

differs from Hegelian Orthodoxy by inverting the main logical sequence, not by discarding the logic or resorting to new tests of truth or finality.... In the materialistic conception, man's spiritual life – what man thinks – is a reflex of what he is in the natural respect, very much in the same fashion as the Orthodox Hegelian would make the natural world a reflex of the spirit. ... But in both cases some fact of creative primacy is assigned to one or the other member of the complex, and in neither case is the relation between the two members a causal relation. In both, the dominant form of speculation and formulation of theory is the conception of movement, development, evolution, progress; and in both, the movement is conceived necessarily to take place by the method of conflict and struggle. The movement is of the nature of progress – gradual advance toward a goal toward the realization in explicit form of all that is implicit in the substantial activity involved in the movement. The movement is further, self-conditioned and self-acting: it is an unfolding by inner necessity.

The Hegelian and the Natural Right (or utilitarian) origins of the Marxian system have been noted by others. The Hegelian metaphysic is identified with the class struggle, the utilitarian element with the labour theory of value. Indeed, many critics of Marx have been 'led to deny the Marxian system all substantial originality, and make it a (doubtfully legitimate) offshoot of English Liberalism and natural rights'. But this is their mistake.

It is scarcely worthwhile to question what serves as the beginning of wisdom in the current criticism of Marx; namely that he offers no adequate proof of his labor-value theory. It is even safe to go further and say that he offers no proof of it.

. . .

The feint which occupies the opening paragraphs of the *Kapital* and the corresponding passages of *Zur Kritik*, etc., is not to be taken seriously as an attempt to prove his position on this head [the labour theory of value] by the ordinary recourse to argument. It is rather a self-satisfied superior's playful mystification of those (critics) whose limited powers do not enable them to see that his proposition is self-evident. Taken on the Hegelian (neo-Hegelian) ground, and seen in the light of the general materialistic conception, the proposition that value-labor cost is self-evident, not to say tautological, seen in any other light, it has no particular force.

'In the Hegelian scheme of things the very substantial reality is the unfolding life of the spirit.' Goods 'are the output of this unfolding life of man, a material residue embodying a given fraction of this forceful life-process'. '. . . the metaphysical substance of life – labor power' is embodied in goods and only labour power can give value, for that *is* value. Thus, economists' criticisms of Marx were not incorrect in showing that Marx's labour theory of value is inconsistent with the utilitarian premise. Their critique is simply irrelevant, since the labour theory of value relates not to the utilitarian but, rather, to the Hegelian metaphysical premises. 'The theory of value, then, is *contained in* the main postulates of the Marxian system rather than derived from them.'

Strangely enough, the utilitarian premises provide the basis for the class struggle which has been mistakenly identified with Hegelianism. The class struggle

is in fact a piece of Hedonism, and is related to Bentham rather than to Hegel. . . . The struggle is asserted to be a conscious one, and proceeds on a recognition by the competing classes of their mutually incompatible interests with regard to the material means of life. The class struggle proceeds on motives of interest, and a recognition of class interest can, of course, be reached only by reflection on the facts of the case.

It is not materialistic at all. It is a 'sequence of reflection' and 'consequent choice of sides to a quarrel'.

Thus, having shown the conventional criticism irrelevant, Veblen argues the inconsistency of Marx's conclusions to his materialistic premises. A truly materialistic interpretation, he says,

> would have led, as Darwinism has, to a concept of a process of cumulative change in social structure and function; but this process, being essentially a cumulative sequence of causation, opaque and unteleological, could not, without an infusion of pious fancy by the speculator, be asserted to involve progress as distinct from retrogression or to tend to a 'realization' or 'self-realization' of the human spirit or of anything else.

One can summarize by saying that the Marxian theory of value was, in Veblen's opinion, simply a tautology resting on mysterious Hegelian premises of an unfolding life force. Marx's class struggle, on the other hand, is 'a specious bit of Hedonism', imputing interest even to whole classes of people. And finally, a consistently materialistic revision of Marx would necessarily eliminate his inevitable progression to a classless state.

In a second article, Veblen sweeps the field of Marx's 'followers'. With scarcely concealed contempt, he relates how they attempt to reinterpret the obsolete Hegelian metaphysics in terms of the intrinsically incompatible Darwinism, and how they squirm under the resurgence of nationalism. What he said of the German branch may be taken as his opinion of the whole: 'The leaders are busy with interpretations of their earlier formulations. They have come to excite themselves over nebulous distinctions between patriotism and jingoism.'

Veblen's analysis is, of course, complicated by the fact that he criticizes Marx, Marx's critics and Marx's followers from a standpoint of a materialistic Darwinism, which is itself untenable.

3. 'ON THE INTELLECTUAL PRE-EMINENCE OF THE JEWS IN MODERN EUROPE'[6]

In 1919 Veblen finished an article growing out of a luncheon conversation with the editor of a Zionist magazine. The editor advanced the idea that once the Jews found a homeland free of the oppression and prejudice of Gentile culture, their natural and cultural superiority, already evident under these repressive conditions in Europe, would blossom into an epoch of scientific and cultural achievement. The editor commissioned Veblen to write this theory up. Veblen's final product was, characteristically, the opposite of what the editor expected. Veblen argued that it is neither the racial nor the cultural superiority of the Jews which accounts for their exceptionally disproportionate contributions to scientific and cultural development. Rather, he says, it is the fact that they have lived in a basically alien Gentile culture. Thus, when the Zionist ideal is attained, when the Jews create their own integrated, consistent life-style, unprovoked by alien disturbances, they will lose their advantage and sink into the sands of conventional respectability like everyone else.

Veblen's analysis of the intellectual attributes of the Jews is of interest in itself; it is also interesting as an interpretation of the methods of scientific inquiry (quite different from the inductivism attributed to institutionalism). Lastly, it is interesting as an intellectual autobiography. One could easily replace the word 'Jew' with old-world 'Norwegian' and discover the source of that peculiar 'man from Mars' flavour of Veblen himself.

First, on scientific method:

The first requisite for constructive work in modern science, and indeed for any work of inquiry that shall bring enduring results, is a skeptical frame of mind. . . . Much good and serviceable workmanship of a workaday character goes into the grand total of modern scientific achievement; but that pioneering and engineering work of guidance, design, and theoretical correlation, without which the most painstaking collection and canvass of information is irrelevant, incompetent, and impertinent – this intellectual enterprise that goes forward presupposes a degree of exemption from hard-and-fast preconceptions, a skeptical animus, *Unbefangenheit*, release from the dead hand of conventional finality.

Thus,

The intellectually gifted Jew is in a peculiarly fortunate position in respect of this requisite immunity from the inhibitions of intellectual quietism. But he can come in for such immunity only at the cost of losing his secure place in the scheme of conventions into which he has been born, and at the cost, also, of finding no similarly secure place in that scheme of gentile con-

ventions into which he is thrown. For him as for other men in
the like case, the skepticism that goes to make him an effectual
factor in the increase and diffusion of knowledge among men
involves a loss of the peace of mind that is the birthright of the
safe and sane quietist. He becomes a disturber of the intellectual
peace, but only at the cost of becoming an intellectual wayfar-
ing man, a wanderer in the intellectual no-man's-land, seeking
another place to rest, farther along the road, somewhere over
the horizon. They are neither a complaisant nor a contented
lot, these aliens of the uneasy feet; but that is, after all, not the
point in question.

. . .

Intellectually he is likely to become an alien; spiritually he is
more than likely to remain a Jew; for the heartstrings of affection and consuetude are tied early, and they are not readily
retied in after life. Nor does the animus with which the community of safe and sane gentiles is wont to meet him conduce at
all to his personal incorporation in that community, whatever
may befall the intellectual assets which he brings. Their people
need not become his people nor their gods his gods, and indeed
the provocation is forever and irritably present all over the
place to turn back from following after them. The most amiable
share in the gentile community's life that is likely to fall to his
lot is that of being interned.

Therefore, realization of the Zionist homeland will perhaps
bring 'some gain to the repatriated Children of Israel', but 'some
losses to Christendom at large. . . . It is a sufficiently difficult
choice between a life of complacent futility at home and a thank-
less quest of unprofitable knowledge abroad.'

For, again – and this is a fitting end to a discussion of Veblenia
– 'One who goes away from home will come to see many unfamiliar things, and to take note of them; but it does not follow that he
will swear by all the strange gods whom he meets along the road.'

5 Veblen's Social Theory

It is impossible to understand Veblen's social theory without first attempting to understand his problem. This problem was, in its most elemental terms, the problem of free will versus determinism. Veblen not only failed to solve this problem – a failure for which he can hardly be blamed; but he refused to 'choose up sides', to create a consistent theory based on one or the other of these premises, and his fence-straddling over this issue was inexcusable.

Thus even the title of this chapter is incorrect. Veblen had two mutually contradictory theories and an interpretation based on one of the theories may easily be refuted by citations derived from the other. An interpretation based on either theory alone necessarily becomes a straw man.

Naturally, in such a situation where there are two Veblens, one is led to search for some consistent theme or cause. After all, Veblen had the right to change his mind. Something of the sort indeed seems to have happened, although the following account is necessarily somewhat impressionistic.

From the time of Veblen's 'Why is Economics not an Evolutionary Science?' in 1898, through to, at least, 'The Limitations of Marginal Utility' in 1909, Veblen was preoccupied with matters of methodology. He began, in the earlier article, with a very promising attack on the hedonism of mainstream economics which he found epitomized in the marginal utility analysis of Karl Menger and the Austrian school.[1] Even if one thinks Veblen's description of utilitarianism is inaccurate, it certainly is a wonderful caricature:

The hedonistic conception of man is that of a lightning calculator of pleasures and pains, who oscillates like a homogeneous globule of desire of happiness under the impulse of stimuli that shift him about the area, but leave him intact. He has neither antecedent nor consequent. He is an isolated, definitive human datum, in stable equilibrium except for the buffets of the impinging forces that displace him in one direction or another. Self-imposed in elemental space, he spins symmetrically about his own spiritual axis until the parallelogram of forces bears down upon him, whereupon he follows the line of the resultant. When the force of the impact is spent, he comes to rest, a self-contained globule of desire as before.[2]

Veblen contends that man 'is not simply a bundle of desires that are to be saturated by being placed in the path of the forces of the environment, but rather a coherent structure of propensities and habits which seeks realization and expression in an unfolding activity'.[3]

This statement stands squarely in the finest tradition of humanism and one can only wonder how Veblen failed to see this same heroic conception of man in those he attacked. For example, the great philosopher of utilitarianism, John Stuart Mill, said the same thing, only better (one of the few instances when this statement can be made with regard to any author in comparison with Veblen):

I never, indeed, wavered in the conviction that happiness is the test of all rules of conduct, and the end of life. But I now thought that this end was only to be attained by not making it the direct end. Those only are happy (I thought) who have their minds fixed on some object other than their own happiness; on the happiness of others, on the improvement of mankind, even on some art or pursuit, followed not as a means, but as itself an ideal and, aiming thus at something else, they find happiness by the way.[4]

In the above objection to hedonism Veblen is clearly on the side of 'free will' – of the humanists. But even in this early article there is discernible the faint tune of determinism cast in the rubric of an evolutionary theory of human conduct. This tendency grows through the next decade of his writings, culminating in the highly deterministic and behaviouristic theory put forward in his classic essay, 'The Place of Science in Modern Civilization' (1906), and methodologically explicated in 'The Limitations of Marginal Utility' in 1908.

In the latter work there are ten pages[5] which epitomize the two

Veblens. One can hardly believe it is the same author one is reading, much less the same essay of the same author.

Veblen begins by criticizing hedonistic economics for embracing the methodology of 'sufficient reason' rather than the methodology of 'efficient cause' characteristic of the physical sciences:

> The difference may seem trivial. It is serious only in its consequences. *The two methods of inference – from sufficient reason and from efficient cause – are out of touch with one another and there is no transition from one to the other: no method of converting the procedure or the results of the one into those of the other.* The immediate consequence is that the resulting economic theory is of a teleological character – 'deductive' or 'a priori' as it is often called – instead of being drawn in terms of cause and effect. The relation sought by this theory among the facts with which it is occupied is the control exercised by future (apprehended) events over present conduct. Current phenomena are dealt with as conditioned by their future consequences; and in strict marginal-utility theory they can be dealt with only in respect of their control of the present by consideration of the future. Such a (logical) relation of control or guidance between the future and the present of course involves an exercise of intelligence, a taking thought, and hence an intelligent agent through whose discriminating forethought the apprehended future may affect the current course of events; unless, indeed, one were to admit something in the way of a providential order of nature or some occult line of stress of the nature of sympathetic magic. Barring magical and providential elements, the relation of sufficient reason runs by way of the interested discrimination, the forethought, of an agent who takes thought of the future and guides his present activity by regard for this future. The relation of sufficient reason runs only from the (apprehended) future into the present, and it is solely of an intellectual, subjective, personal, teleological character and force; while the relation of cause and effect runs only in the contrary direction, and it is solely of an objective, impersonal, materialistic character and force. The modern scheme of knowledge, on the whole, rests, for its definitive ground, on the relation of cause and effect; the relation of sufficient reason being admitted only provisionally and as a proximate factor in

the analysis, always with the unambiguous reservation that the analysis must ultimately come to rest in terms of cause and effect.[6]

Given the italicized portions of the above quotation and neglecting the equivocation towards the end, it seems that Veblen here realized he had to choose between humanism and behaviourism and that he was prepared to choose the latter. But this does not happen. The subsequent paragraph reaffirms choice and rationality in human conduct. Indeed, he reaffirms, in this discussion, a crucially important earlier footnote which shows that Veblen realized *precisely* why the method of efficient cause is inappropriate in the study of humans:

> The conduct of mankind differs from that of the brutes in being determined by *anticipated* sensations of pleasure and pain, instead of *actual* sensations. Hereby, in so far, human conduct is taken out of the sequence of cause and effect and falls instead under the rule of sufficient reason. By virtue of this rational faculty in man the connection between stimulus and response is teleological instead of causal.[7]

Finally, Veblen, torn between these two incommensurate theories, attempts a compromise. Men choose, but the purposes upon which the choice is made are determined by the cultural milieu, by the forces of habituation:

> To any modern scientist interested in economic phenomena, the chain of cause and effect in which any given phase of human culture is involved, as well as the cumulative changes wrought in the fabric of human conduct itself by the habitual activity of mankind, are matters of more engrossing and more abiding interest than the method of inference by which an individual is presumed invariably to balance pleasure and pain under given conditions that are presumed to be normal and invariable. The former are questions of the life-history of the race or the community, questions of cultural growth and of the fortunes of generations; while the latter is a question of individual casuistry in the face of a given situation that may arise in the course of this cultural growth. The former bear on the continuity and mutations of that scheme of conduct whereby mankind deals with its material means of life; the latter, if it is conceived in

hedonistic terms, concerns a disconnected episode in the sensuous experience of an individual member of such a community.[8]

In this characteristic statement, Veblen teeters between free will and determinism, humanism and behaviourism, in a clear attempt to have his cake and eat it too. He criticized mainstream economics for construing man as a mere automaton – responding only to the impinging forces of his environment. Yet he also criticizes this same economics for being premised on purpose, for employing the method of sufficient reason! Then, when Veblen turned to the construction of his own theory, his first act was to make choice a mere illusion, choices being determined by culture, thus embracing an evolutionary mechanism of 'efficient cause'! In order to support this mechanism he clearly realized that his psychological premise must be that of a materialistic behaviourism. Yet Veblen, more than any other, sensed that the problems of perception and anticipation in human conduct pose insurmountable barriers to this psychology.[9]

By 1914, with the publication of *The Instinct of Workmanship and the State of the Industrial Arts*, Veblen felt he had found a solution to these problems. He had worked on the book for over ten years and personally considered it his best work. The solution is implicit in the title. On the one hand are certain universal instincts shared by all men. On the other hand are habits of thought and institutions variable among people depending on time and place. The instincts give direction and force to the process of human development; the habits give the specific content of the moment. Thus, one culture may practise witchcraft, the other science, but they are both employed in these pursuits by the instinct of workmanship (or the idle curiousity). Veblen then accounts for the evolution of the habitual, the specifically cultural features of human society, in terms of its economic base – in terms, that is, of the state of the industrial arts. Thus, sufficient reason becomes wedded to efficient cause in a new synthesis. Veblen's social theory, outlined below, can only be understood in the context of his attempt to achieve this resolution of his methodological problems.

There is no better place to begin a discussion of Veblen's social theory than, as it were, at the very bottom, with his treatment of the role of instincts in human behaviour. As Veblen uses 'instinct' in a very special way, it is profitable to spend some time getting this usage clearly in mind.

The biological characteristics of man, Veblen says, impose two separate constraints on his behaviour. First, there are those innate factors whose operations produce an 'aimless but unwavering response to stimulus'; these Veblen terms 'tropisms', and the behaviour or act engendered by their operation, 'tropismatic reactions':

> The recognized tropisms stand out, to all appearance, as sharply defined physiological traits, transmissible by inheritance intact and unmodified, separable and unblended, in a manner suggestively like the 'unit characters' spoken of in latter-day theories of heredity.[10]

The tropisms are, to Veblen, those immediate and unreflecting physiological reactions to stimuli, such as the knee jerk, popular among behaviourists.

But Veblen does not consider tropisms an important element of social theory. They are discussed mainly for purposes of contrast with the important element, in his thinking, the 'instincts'. Veblen's instincts do not directly prescribe a mode of behaviour. Rather they are the biological basis of certain universal human *purposes*:

> These various native proclivities that are so classed together as 'instincts' have the characteristic in common that they all and several, more or less imperatively, propose an objective end of endeavor. On the other hand, what distinguishes one instinct from another is that each sets up a characteristic purpose, aim, or object to be attained, different from the objective end of any other instinct.[11]

The 'tropisms' and the 'instincts' differ, therefore, in this important regard: while the tropisms prescribe the form of the reaction, or the *actual behaviour* exhibited by the agent in response to any given stimulus, they state nothing as to the outcome (intended or realized) of the act; whereas the instincts prescribe nothing as to form of the reaction, but state only the biologically determined ends in view, or the *anticipated outcome* of whatever action takes place. Between tropisms and the instincts, therefore, lies the 'threshold of intelligence':

> Such impulsive action as is in no degree intelligent, and so suffers no adaptation through habitual use, is not properly to be called instinctive; it is rather to be classed as tropismatic.
>
> .   .   .
>
> When instincts enjoin little else than the end of endeavor, leaving the sequence of acts, by which the end is to be approached somewhat a matter of open alternatives, the share of reflection, discretion and deliberate adaptation will be correspondingly large. The range and diversity of habituation is also correspondingly large.[12]

A complete appreciation of the role of instincts in Veblenian analysis must await further development of his theory, but one might now mention the types of instincts Veblen stresses and the way in which they are interpreted. Among the many instinctive proclivities, it is remarkable to reflect how very few have a direct genetic basis. Thus, the 'parental bent' *may* not have a genetic origin at all – it may be simply universal among human cultures because of the love brought by intimate relations within a family. Similarly, Veblen at times implies that even the important 'instinct of workmanship' is not a conventional 'instinct', but rather an 'aptitude' or a 'propensity' for effectual work flowing from man's constitution as an end-seeking organism:

> He is an agent seeking in every act the accomplishment of some concrete, objective, impersonal end. By force of his being such an agent he is possessed of a taste for effective work, and a distaste for futile effort. He has a sense of the merit of serviceability or efficiency and of the demerit of futility, waste or incapacity, this aptitude or propensity may be called the instinct of workmanship.[13]

In this sense it is indeed true, as Wesley Mitchell emphasizes, that Veblen, rather than adopting a naïve instinct-psychology, actually amended the instinctive school by showing how the universality of various propensities is not necessarily an argument in favour of the idea that they are 'instinctively' rooted in the biological constitution of man. They are (in modern terms) 'emergent properties': 'spiritual traits *emerging from* a certain concurrence of physiological unit characters', and not the 'unit characters' themselves.[14]

As the subsequent discussion clearly shows, any emphasis upon instinctive prescription of behaviour *per se* would negate Veblen's own theory. Thus, Veblen goes to great pains to show that the instincts may cancel one another through the sheer force of their contrary pull on the same body; or that the institutional structure of society may suppress or encourage one class of instincts at the expense of another; or that the ultimate ends they prescribe may be forgotten or neglected in pursuit of more proximate ends set up by the habitual backwash of human thought and action.[15]

But there is one instinct in Veblen's classification that is more or less continuous, incorruptible by the exigencies of culture, and that is the 'idle curiosity'. The idle curiosity, Veblen says, is like the 'aptitude for play' observed in children – activity for the sake of activity alone; only in this case the activity is mental and speculative. People wish not only to know about things but also the 'why' of things, and it is this explanatory capacity of the mind which carries thought *beyond* mere sensory impressions and *beyond* the interest in solely expedient conduct into the range of creative intelligence:

> On the human plane, intelligence . . . may throw the response into the form of a reasoned line of conduct looking to an outcome that shall be expedient for the agent. . . . But that is not all. The inhibitive nervous complication may also detach another chain of response to the given stimulus, which does not spend itself in a line of motor conduct and does not fall into a system of uses. Pragmatically speaking, this outlying chain of response is immaterial and irrelevant.[16]

Veblen thus creates a distinction between the 'pragmatic animus' and the 'idle curiosity'; between practical life and thought, and knowledge. Civilization owes nothing to the pragmatic arts, he says, except 'maxims of expedient conduct'. 'In this field there is scarcely a degree of advance from Confucius to Samuel Smiles.'[17] In contrast, the progressive, cumulative change in knowledge due to the insistent drive of the idle curiosity is the root cause of social development and change:

Pragmatism creates nothing but maxims of expedient conduct. Science creates nothing but theories. . . . Wisdom and proficiency of the pragmatic sort does not contribute to the advance of a knowledge of fact. It has only an incidental bearing on scientific research, and its bearing is chiefly that of inhibition and misdirection.[18]

But the idle curiosity is only a part of things; it is the source, not the substance of knowledge. For example, it does not explain the 'evolution of the scientific point of view'. While the idle curiosity has always been present in all cultures through all time, it is only lately, and then only among a comparatively small percentage of the people in a certain area of the globe, that 'science' has occurred at all. These and related considerations lead Veblen out of the instinctive ground of his theory into its truly sociological aspects – to a consideration of the 'habits of thought', scientific and otherwise, and the 'process of habituation' by which these habits of thought come into being:[19]

In what manner and with what effect the idle curiosity of mankind first began to tame the facts thrown in its way, far back in the night of time, and to break them in under a scheme of habitual interpretation; what may have been the earliest norms of systematic knowledge, such as would serve the curiosity of the earliest generations of men in a way analogous to the service rendered the curiosity of later generations by scientific inquiry – all that is, of course, a matter of long-range conjecture more or less wild, which cannot be gone into here.[20]

This is how Veblen chooses to introduce the central factor of his theory.

Veblen discusses the 'process of habituation' as a process through which one experience comes to determine, in a largely unconscious and unreflecting manner, the response to a similar set of stimuli. Habits are a kind of socially determined tropism. Habits can be one of two different kinds. The habit may be a normative *conception* or *criterion* pertaining to the validity, expediency or merit of a given line of conduct and deliberation; or it may be a *usage* or *act* whose expediency or merit is not usually questioned but which is performed impulsively, undeliberatively, automatically by a person or body of persons. The habitual 'conception or criterion' is what Veblen terms a *habit of thought*; the 'usage or act' he terms an *institution*:[21]

> An institution is of the nature of a usage which has become axiomatic and indispensable by habituation and general acceptance. Its physiological counterpart would presumably be any of those habitual addictions that are now attracting the attention of the experts in sobriety.[22]

At this point the development of Veblen's social philosophy reaches an important juncture. The forces of purpose – the instincts, habits of thought, sufficient reason – are aligned against the behaviouristic forces of tropisms, institutions and efficient cause. Veblen encounters the basic problem of the *causality* between thought and action. Briefly, <u>Veblen's theory is that the idle curiosity (thought) creates theories which in turn create technology</u>. The technological mode of the moment imposes a unique discipline on the behaviour of those most closely associated with it. From this disciplined *behaviour* emerges the characteristic habits of thought of the next stage: the notions of the true, the good and the beautiful of an age. Thus, <u>while thought – the idle curiosity – is the *primum mobile* of Veblen's theory, it only affects action and the prevailing habits of thought at the second remove – through the technology it creates.</u> For this reason Veblen's theory cannot be described as truly deterministic because one never knows what the idle curiosity will create. But it is behaviouristic in the strict sense that the technological mode provides a set of unique stimuli (a 'discipline') to which both behaviour and habits of thought respond in a primarily unconscious and unreflecting way. This is the basic structure of the behaviouristic Veblen; it is the predominant Veblen in his formal theory. Other chapters illustrate the 'other' humanistic Veblen, but here the task is to follow the behaviouristic Veblen out to the end:

> It may be taken as a generalization *grounded in the instinctive* endowment of mankind that the human sense of workmanship (or the idle curiosity) will unavoidably go on turning to account what there is in hand of technological knowledge, and so will in the course of time, by insensible gains, perhaps, gradually change the technological scheme and *therefore* also the scheme of customary canons of conduct answering to it. . . .[23]

... habits of thought are the outcome of habits of life ... the discipline of daily life acts to alter or reinforce the ... received institutions under which men live. And the direction in which, on the whole, the alteration proceeds is conditioned by the trend of the discipline of daily life.[24]

Because habits of action determine habits of thought, the term 'institution' need not be restricted to one or the other; Veblen uses the word almost indifferently to mean either 'thought' or 'act'. 'That is what is meant by calling them institutions; they are settled habits of thought common to the generality of men.'[25]

Veblen's theory, like that of Marx, is based upon the technological-economic substratum of society,[26] but he severely takes Marx to task (and thereby reveals the behaviouristic bias of his own theory) for believing that the reason for the importance of the economic base is the 'economic interests' of the classes; as noted before, he considers class interest just another 'piece of Hedonism'. Classes may or may not have 'interests', Veblen says, but whether they do or do not is quite beside the point, as the 'interests' of individuals, groups, classes or whatnot have little or no bearing on the fact of institutional change. Economic activity is the most important, simply because people spend more time in economic activities, and are thus exposed more to characteristic economic *usages*, than to other forms of usage. Thus, when two bodies of thought and usage clash in a community, the question of the eventual outcome of the situation is not a question of the merits or products of the competing systems; it is merely a question of the relative time spent by the community in participating in each:

> It is only that a given individual – call him the common man – will not be occupied with both of these incommensurable systems of logic and appreciation at the same time or bearing on the same point; and further that in proportion as his waking hours and his mental energy are fully occupied within the lines of one of these systems of knowledge, design and employment, in much the same measure he will necessarily neglect the other, and in time he will lose proficiency and interest in its pursuits and conclusions.[27]

Thus, Veblen shuts the door on a rationalistic (in his words 'hedonistic') account of the nature and importance of technology in terms of the opportunities for gain it opens or closes. Rather, the influence is more direct, more primitive; it is a direct flow of causality from technology through 'usage' to thought, in that singular direction. How, precisely, this happens is something that would have to be explained in the same terms as the connection between hammer and knee jerk in behaviourism. Veblen never bothered to advance an explanation and one certainly will not be attempted here. Some 'feel' for the way Veblen thought of this 'opaque', as he carefully called it, causal flow and formal completion of this side of Veblen's theory can be obtained through perusal of his 'stages' of history.

Veblen's intent was to explain 'the evolution of the scientific point of view' in accord with his underlying theory. He discerned four major stages, each corresponding to a characteristic technological mode and accompanying habits of thought.[28]

I. 'MATTER OF FACT IN THE ERA OF SAVAGERY'

The idle curiosity, although an 'instinct', functions only within the scope left it by the absence of pragmatism. As noted before, these are two distinct and mutually exclusive aspects of intelligence. The 'pragmatic animus' looks to things with an eye to their 'conversion to use'; the idle curiosity cares nothing for the use to which things may be put – it is 'curiosity' only, disinterested and purely 'idle'. Its only concern is with the interpretation of events and their explanation in terms that seem right and definitive to the knower.

The prehistoric era of 'savagery' was one marked by comparative peace.[29] While there were conflicts between alien tribes, and also between members within the respective tribes, these conflicts must have been sporadic and half-hearted interruptions of the day-to-day struggle with nature over the terms of existence. The era of savagery was marked by such a low state of development of the industrial arts that most of the time of any given savage was spent on directly productive enterprise – on pain of extinction – not on predatory pursuits and forceful acquisition from others. Besides, 'a life by predation implies something substantial to prey upon', and the crude implements and primitive amenities possessed by savages did not offer much incentive to acquisition where

even a modicum of risk was involved. Thus, the era of savagery
was habitually peaceful and characterized by directly productive
activity.

Theories generated by the idle curiosity in this era reflect the
peaceful state of the savage existence. These theories were
characterized by a rather free-wheeling interpretation of phenomena in terms of primitive animism and sympathetic magic.
These earliest mythologies and legends were almost completely
divorced from the savage's day-to-day existence. They were
wholly 'idle'. The interpretations seized upon satisfied the
curiosity only. Deities were not objects of supplication or considered interest, they were only explanatory. Thus, the idle curiosity was allowed free play and the habits of peace were firmly
ingrained in society in the era of savagery.

2. 'MATTER OF FACT IN THE ERA OF BARBARISM'

The barbarian culture represents a marked change from the older,
savage state of affairs. This era, lasting through the close of the
late Middle Ages, is marked by predation on a vast and unprece-
dented scale. Predatory exploits became the normative standards
of society and whatever was not of this predatory cast – whatever
was productive and non-invidious – was not considered honour-
able or even tolerable in the eyes of society. Those who lived a life
by predation were considered the worthy, desired and noble
members of society; while those directly concerned with production entertained no wish so fervent as to lose their plebeian
origins in a life of unremitting theft.

The barbarian life bred a strong proclivity for the pragmatic
appreciation of things. The pragmatic animus obtruded into hori-
zons previously tended by idle curiosity. The interpretation of
events was performed with an eye open to the main chance. The
terms of interpretation also assumed this barbarian cast. The force,
prepotency and might imputed to phenomena supplanted the
older savage terms of motive and propensity, and the elements of
nature were arranged in a feudalistic array of 'graded rank and
dignity' – after the fashion of alchemy and astronomy.

This accentuated pragmatism, while sterile in itself, focused the
barbarian attention on matters of fact. Matters of fact were conceived under the pragmatic animus as objects of use and expedient

gain, and thus afford no contribution to real knowledge. But attention, under pragmatism, is rooted firmly in the consideration of reality, of the here and now. This habitual concern with reality remained after the withering away of pragmatism.

3. 'CAUSALITY IN THE ERA OF HANDICRAFT'

In the era of handicraft, the craftsman, the small businessman and the itinerant merchant come into greater prominence in the society. These respective pursuits required a sedulous attention to detail and an appreciation of objective causal forces at work in the given situation. The craftsman, especially, came to appreciate the conditions imposed by his tools and materials upon the objects of his pursuit. He learned to combine tools in functional patterns, and his attention was habitually riveted upon the causal forces at work as he applied 'skill, dexterity and judgment' to the fashioning of goods.

Under handicraft norms, the barbarian considerations of inherent force and propensity in materials (alchemy) give way to ideas of dexterous control over causal processes. The craftsman entered, in his own appreciation, as an efficient cause into the situation and, through his dexterity, was able to attain an objective effect in the form of a product.

Theoretical interpretation in terms of cause and effect is thus of handicraft origin. Although the preconception of cause and effect is not, Veblen says, an essential ingredient of modern science, its connotations and presumptions underlie and condition the course of scientific inquiry. Scientists rely upon a concept of causality, or activity, imputed to the phenomena and they do not consider the inquiry completed until a cause-and-effect sequence is linked between the items of theoretical concern. Thus, 'action at a distance' is repugnant to scientific theory; that is, no causal 'influence' is imputed to one factor over another unless there is some direct contact, or contact through a continuum, between the two factors. The era of handicraft emerges with a semi-animistic idea of direct cause and effect. This idea is later reduced to a concept of 'opaque' cause and effect governing the action of a sequence of concatenation of cumulative change.

4. 'SEQUENCE AND THE MACHINE TECHNOLOGY'

As the state of the industrial arts matured to a form approaching that of the present day, its implementation required an elaborate and complex network of interacting sequences in the form of machine technology. It outgrew the simple image of the handi-craftsman and his tools and came to rely upon forces, masses, velocities, strengths and the like. The machine process is not a process of individual causes working given effects, as in handicraft; it is rather a process of small incremental changes being worked in materials that lead to a cumulative result in the finished product. Machine technology de-emphasizes the notion of individual causes working given effects and fosters in its stead a concept of 'opaque' cause and effect, of cumulative change working through an active process to turn out a product which is simply the last incremental mark of the whole sequence. This stage is the present phase of the 'evolution of the scientific point of view' – the disinterested explanation of matters of fact in terms of processes of cumulative change.

As these stages show, there is in Veblen, as in Marx, an intimate connection between the technological means and the economic mode. Capitalism arose out of the handicraft era, but may be obsolete in the era of machine process. Veblen at times felt that contemporary technology may occasion a drift to socialism. But here he differed from Marx in refusing to embrace a deterministic 'historicist' attitude:

> It is quite impossible on Darwinian grounds to foretell whether the 'proletariat' will go on to establish the socialist revolution or turn aside again, and sink their force in the broad sands of patriotism. It is a question of habit and native propensity and of the range of stimuli to which the proletariat are exposed and are to be exposed, and what may be the outcome is not a matter of logical consistency but of response to stimulus.[30]

Wesley C. Mitchell well encapsulated the essence of Veblen's theory:

> His evolutionary theory forbids him to anticipate a cataclysm, or to forecast a millennium. What will happen in the inscrutable

future is what has been happening since the origin of man. As ways of working shift, they will engender new habits of thinking, which will crystallize into new institutions, which will form the cultural setting for further cumulative changes in ways of working, world without end.[31]

This completes the discussion of the one – the behaviouristic – Veblen. It would be misleading to pretend that this side of Veblen stands out in his own works as graphically as portrayed here.

That there are two Veblens, that he can be interpreted in either one of two internally consistent ways, is shown in the following statement, which is not only an excellent précis of Veblen's thought, but surely one of the grandest sentences of all social theory:

The growth of culture is a cumulative sequence of habituation, and the ways and means of it are the habitual response of human nature to exigencies that very incontinently, cumulatively, but with something of a consistent sequence in the cumulative variations that so go forward – incontinently – because each new move creates a new situation which induces a further new variation in the habitual manner of response; cumulatively, because each new situation is a variation of what has gone before it and embodies as causal factors all that has been effected by what went before; consistently, because the underlying traits of human nature (propensities, aptitudes, and whatnot) by force of which the response takes place, and on ground of which the habituation takes effect, remain substantially unchanged.[32]

6 Technologism and Behaviourism in C. E. Ayres and M. A. Copeland

The chapter on selected Veblenia presents a sampling of what, in the author's opinion, represents the best of Veblen. This chapter presents the worst. Veblen himself was too sly to develop his methodological prescriptions and the behaviouristic side of his social theory to their full extent. His studied neglect is more than compensated by two of his disciples – the authors under discussion – whose candour and rigour illustrate in sharp relief the path Veblen tentatively explored, but down which he refused to go.

No attempt is made in this chapter to give a comprehensive or balanced view of the works of either Ayres or Copeland. They are of interest here only in so far as they provide examples of a particular tendency in institutionalism. Even their position in this respect is not fully developed; the selections from their work are more on the order of a sampling of what the reader can pursue further on his own if he is so inclined.

The quotations in this chapter of samplings are many and they run to excessive lengths. The reason is that Ayres and Copeland, in their more heroic moments, are almost unquotable, and one who nevertheless quotes them is subject to accusations of taking them 'out of context', and creating 'straw men'. Redundancy and length are thus justified. If, after these efforts, a critic would say, 'You do not understand what these authors *really mean*,' the only possible reply is, 'Perhaps not, but that is what they *really say*.'

As someone observed, Ayres out-Veblens Veblen and out-Deweys Dewey. With respect to the three basic elements in Veblen's original analysis – individuals, institutions and technology – Ayres reduces the individuals to institutions and the institutions, in turn, to technology. Individuals and their (alleged) purposes thus become little more than a circuit through which the substantial current of causation passes directly between technology and the behavioural patterns whose reflex they are.

Ayres lists as primary among the fallacious holdovers from the past in economic theory 'the disposition of economists to abstract "motives" from other patterns of behaviour; and to think of these as being somehow aboriginal, a sort of well-spring . . . from which all the rest of economic activity flows.'[1] These preconceptions of economists, he says, render the theory 'subjective' and 'mental-istic' – wholly out of keeping with the objective methods of science:

> This is what it means to speak of classical economic theory as 'deductive' reasoning. Obviously there is nothing amiss with deduction . . . [but] The trouble with the classical way of think-ing is its basic propositions, the theory of human 'nature' of which all economic theory is conceived to be the 'natural' expression.[2]

This statement may be interpreted as meaning that economists are wrong only in assigning certain natural and invariant proper-ties to an 'economic man'. It is not the method of assigning motives that is wrong, but merely that the wrong motives are assigned. This doubt is quickly dispelled as soon as Ayres turns to the consideration of the individual in relation to institutions. Thus, he says, culture is 'a phenomenon *sui generis*' and 'this is to deny that social patterns derive from or can be explained in terms of the behavior of "individuals" '.[3]

It is interesting to note how the simple fact of Ayres' writing at a later date than Veblen clarifies the issues. Ayres is able to com-pare behaviourism and rationalism explicitly and directly: 'Insti-tutionalism has been identified with behaviorism as long and as consistently as it has been identified at all; and over the entire span of this association has been a source of general puzzlement.'[4] Ayres wishes to clear this confusion: 'Human beings are social phenomena. Social patterns are not the logical consequents of individual acts; individuals, and all their actions, are the logical consequents of social patterns.'[5] Having disposed of the individual by making him a function of institutions, Ayres turns to the dis-position of institutions by rendering them, in turn, a function of technology. In order to do this he sees quite clearly that he must divorce institutions from any positive, causal effect upon the development of technology.

Institutions are 'permissive' only of technological growth. While they may at times halt it or obstruct it through their sheer 'dead weight', they cannot aid or conduce to its advance except by keeping out of the way. Thus, he addresses a famous question in economic history:

> Did institutions such as those of business enterprise, democracy, Puritanism, and the like 'make possible' the development of the industrial economy? That has been the traditional belief. There is a sense in which that belief is true. But there is a more important sense in which it is quite false. The difference is between active and passive agents. If the institutional structure which prevailed in Western Europe prior to the industrial revolution of the past five centuries or so had been sufficiently solid and rigid to inhibit technological change, then it goes without saying that the change would not have occurred. Since the industrial revolution did occur, obviously the institutional structure which it confronted was *insufficiently solid to prevent change*. That structure was a causally significant part of the total situation; but its significance was – and consequently is still – permissive, not dynamic.[6]

Ayres also replied to a criticism by Frank H. Knight that institutionalism involves 'some . . . absolute and inscrutable type of "causality" by which technology drags behind it and "determines" other phases of social change'. Ayres replied, '. . . ceremonial behavior of its own character invariably simulates, and in this sense follows, technological activity'. Given the line of causality postulated, the 'cultural lag' follows as a matter of course. 'In the process of social change a "drag" of some sort is a matter of common observation.'[7]

With the observation that institutions 'simulate' or 'follow' or 'drag' behind technology, Ayres approaches both the conclusion of his theory and a contradiction highly reminiscent of Veblen's own problems. As the institutions follow technology, and as individuals follow institutions, they both 'lag' behind technology; and *therefore* individuals cannot have much of a hand in the development of technology, for they, being the reflex of institutions, are the *result* of technology. It must be said that Ayres has the fortitude to embrace this consequence with much less equivocation than Veblen. He imbues technology with a kind of sexual propensity and sends it out into the world to proliferate and multiply. The development of technology is not an attribute of 'the skill-faculty of the human individual' but is implicit 'in the character of tools':

It is the peculiar character of all technology, from chipped flints to Boulder Dam and Beethoven's quartets, that it is progressive. It is inherently developmental. This circumstance which gives technology its peculiar importance in the analysis of culture – and most of all for economists – also can be understood only in terms of tools. If we limit the conception of technology to 'skill', we are at once subject to great risk of conceiving technological development as the growth of skills; and since skill is a 'faculty' of 'individuals' we are preconditioned to think of the growth of skill as in some sense an increase of this faculty on the part of individuals. But we know nothing of any such increase.

That is what makes it so hard for economists of the traditional way of thinking to understand the technological principle. . . . Since Veblen first began to write, it has been apparent that some sort of claim was being made for technology as a master-principle of economic analysis. This claim was seen to rest on the peculiarly dynamic character of technology as itself inherently progressive and the agent of social change, in particular the agent of industrial revolution. . . . The whole issue between old and new ways of thinking in economics comes to focus here. The new way of thinking does indeed rest on some kind of inner law of progress. But there is nothing absolute or inscrutable about it. What makes it seem inscrutable is the inveterate predisposition of orthodox economists to think in terms of a conception of human nature as that of the uniquely individual 'spirit'. Thinking so, they think of technology as a skill-faculty of the individual spirit; and thinking so, they find the principle of technological development quite inscrutable – as indeed they must. *For the developmental character of technology is implicit not in the skill-faculty of the human individual but in the character of tools.* The whole analysis must proceed on the level of generalization of culture rather than of individuality in order for the principle of technological progress to be understood at all.[8]

With the notion that technology is not a matter of the 'skill-faculty of the human individual' but 'of tools', the technological reduction is virtually complete. Only one element remains to clear appreciation of the reduction, and that is the concrete way in which tools are assumed to grow and change, independent of any essential contributions on the part of human beings. This, Ayres says quite naturally, is simply a matter of 'accumulation' or 'contact'. Technological advance occurs by virtue of the sheer accumulation of technical materials:[9] 'It is a direct result of the *physical embodiment* of technical behavior patterns in *tools* and *physical materials*.'[10] Thus, it is alleged, the development of agriculture occasioned the development of towns, which in turn piled tools up in one place where they could readily combine into new tools. Thus, also, trade – a consequence of towns and tools of transportation – brought Viking ships into conjunction with certain sailing techniques of the Mediterranean, resulting (more or less directly) in the discovery of America:

> ... this may serve to emphasize two points: that the combination was not deliberate and had no special 'end' in view (such as the Indies), and that a ship is not one simple device but rather a mass of culture traits, so that combination would almost inevitably be the slow function of a general amalgamation and general technological development. But it seems to be a fairly safe conjecture that the age of voyage and discovery was a function of ships. ...[11]

As the number of separate tools grows, the greater by far grows the possible (i.e. necessary) number of combinations. This is 'the technological dynamic':

> We have learned that such technical innovations come about as a result of the physical character of tools which, like all physical objects, are capable of being combined. We know with certainty that inventions and discoveries are combinations of tools, instruments, and instrumentally manipulated materials, and that the more tools there are, the greater is the potentiality of technical invention and discovery.[12]

Lest the term 'potentiality' be taken too seriously, one should note

> the existence in all culture of a dynamic force. A phase of culture which is in itself and of its own character innovational, one in which change is continuous and cumulative and always in the same direction, that of more numerous and more complex technological devices.[13]

And lastly, 'We have here the explanation of the "inscrutable" propensity of all technological devices to proliferate. This "propensity" is a characteristic *not of men but of tools*.'[14]

It should be noted that Ayres at times denies the strict technological determinism of his theory. Thus, he says:

> .... briefly, the theory is that technology (including science) is the dynamic force by which modern civilization (and even, perhaps, all civilization) has been shaped. This is not to say that technology is an external force, external either to human behavior or to social structure. Most emphatically it is not, though much of the misunderstanding of institutionalism derives from the supposition that it is.[15]

Ayres very likely means by this that (as above) institutions can stop progress or hinder it, not that they promote it. But is it possible to assert that if he does not mean this – if he means that institutions can *promote* technological progress – does he contradict his theory? This is the crucial question.

Here again, the discussion must turn to the hopelessly scholastic examination of the meaning of words. The term 'tool' is often used in a broad context meaning 'concepts' – as in Joan Robinson's famous 'bag of tools' in economic analysis. Is this what Ayres means by 'tools'? If so, why, in the numerous instances cited above, does he prefix this term with the adjective 'physical' – as, e.g., 'technical innovations come about as a result of the *physical* character of tools which, like all *physical* objects, are capable of being combined'. But again, in another citation, certainly 'Beethoven's quartets', though tools, cannot be 'physical'; can they not then be 'combined'? Certainly, if 'tools' are used in this broad sense of 'concepts' or 'ideas', some sense could be made of Ayres' assertion that 'the development character of technology is implicit not in the skill-faculty of the human individual but in the character of tools'. This statement could then be taken as meaning that 'intelligence' does not grow over time – only concepts. If this is all that Ayres means, one wonders that he needs several books in which to say it; indeed, that he bothers to mention it at all!

One may speculate that as Veblen's own thinking tended to evolve away from a materialistic behaviourism towards a humanistic interpretation based on instinctive purposes, Ayres' thinking tended in the opposite direction. Ayres intuitively sensed that if technology were to be permitted to be a product of the 'idle curiosity' – of thinking and problem-solving by individuals – the whole edifice of Veblen's theory would be indelibly tainted by humanism – by the method of sufficient reason. Ayres took great pains to purge this intellectualist taint from the foundations of the theory – the technological dynamic. Thus, in Ayres, technology becomes not a product of *concepts*, but rather of 'technical behavior patterns' implicit in 'tools and physical material'.

The opening paragraph in Copeland's very remarkable essay, 'Psychology and the Natural Science Point of View',[16] addresses the question:

Is Psychology a natural science? Can the psychologist deal adequately and satisfactorily with his subject by natural science methods and on natural science assumptions alone? These and the correlative questions for the social sciences are the fundamental issues in the anthropological studies today. They underlie the controversy between those who hold 'purpose' to be a fundamental category of psychology and the stimulus–response psychologists, the controversy between the Gestalt and emergent evolution theorists and the more analytical psychologists, and the controversy between introspectionist and behaviourist.

He says psychology is a natural science, for it is obvious '(a) that a man is a special case of living organism, and (b) that a living organism is a special case of physical object – a special type of complex of electrons and protons'. He then goes on to note an analogy between what might have happened in physiology, and what actually happens in the 'anthropological sciences' – which in turn accounts for the success of the former and the poverty of the latter.

One might speak, Copeland says, of the 'function of the

stomach', or of any other organ in the body, and indeed physiologists speak so, as when such functions are disrupted. But the physiologist does not pretend to explain anything by noting the function of an organ; if it malfunctions, this is not due the obstinacy of the organ. 'Function' has no relation to 'functioning' in the physiological scheme, and the explanation of a function is cast wholly in terms of elements divorced of purpose. So it is, or so it ought to be, in psychology and the social sciences: '... both "behaviourism" and "institutionalism" have been ... used to designate the natural science type of theory in psychology and in social science respectively'.

Copeland's idea is that the human body, at any given instant of time, is composed of certain select complexes among the 'nerve receptors', which determine a characteristic response to corresponding elements in the material world. Some of these complexes the individual is born with, some he acquires by learning or 'conditioning', some are 'dominant' and others latent. Each carries a unique alignment of the receptor nerve patterns, and learning involves a realignment of these patterns. Although this is not too clear, one may assume that the process of learning and the process of bringing complexes to the fore as 'dominant' is an evolutionary process in the biological sense. That is to say, those alignments of the nerve receptors most responsive to the current material situation become dominant through their (comparatively) more frequent use, much as a muscle becomes stronger through exercise (Veblen's 'patterns of usage').

Thus, what some might call 'learning' is the 'substitution of one set of receptors for another', which behaviourists term 'conditioning or association – a new set of receptors and a new or substitute stimulus may come to be associated with a given effector pattern, by repeated presentation of old and new stimuli together'.

Copeland, as would be expected, offers no behaviouristic explanation of any given concrete example. He confines himself exclusively to showing how an explanation would run *if* he would (or could!) do it. But he does take some remarkably simple examples and uses them as devices illustrative of certain methodological prescriptions that a behaviouristic explanation should and/or would satisfy. Thus, Copeland insists:

... a 'responsive-pattern' is not to be defined in terms of results, as 'stirring one's coffee'. These procedures lead to teleological interpretations rather than scientific descriptive generalization. The response-pattern is stirring one's coffee with the spoon in the right hand and with a very special type of position and movement of that hand and arm.

He also insists, with heavy-handed methodological rigour, that when examining S's stopping his automobile at the signal 'red', one must bear in mind that even if the subject says he stopped because of a red 'sensation' or something, 'it was presumably the stimulus and not S's condition (mental state, if you prefer) that was red'. One must explain stopping the automobile through the presence of light-waves of a certain frequency and apparently not in terms of the threat of a traffic summons.

It is interesting to note that although Copeland discusses 'perception' for three pages in this short essay, he does not particularly regard it as a problem. At least he does not address the problem as to how *one element* out of the *infinite* numbers of elements in the material situation serves as a stimulus. Thus, he assumes away what is surely his major problem – the problem of 'awakeness or awareness':

> We may speak of the group of response-patterns which are on the threshold of readiness to function at any one time, i.e. not 'inhibited', as a dominant complex of response patterns, and a stimulus which calls out any of these responses as being in the focus of attention or awakeness or awareness.

Copeland returns to his methodological ideas with a reminder of the necessity of serial, temporal causation; and a caution to his fellow-behaviourists against mere sophistry. He notes that the main thing is always to explain the act as the precedent determining the consequent, not, as in rationalism, the other way around. He goes on to note that many behaviourists fall into the mistake of thinking that they change the analysis just through a change in words:

> . . . 'telic' designates behavior in which antecedent responses appear to be determined by the consequent 'end'. The word 'teleological' applies to terms or statements which imply that consequent does determine antecedent in telic behavior. It is

sometimes felt that to describe telic behavior in non-teleological terms is to deprive it of its telic character.

However, this admonition apparently does not apply to Copeland himself. For on the next page he indulges in a classic of behaviouristic sophistry. Commensurate with the requirement that behaviour is to be construed as proceeding from antecedent to consequent, Copeland translates 'ends' or 'desires' into 'drives', thus making behaviour a kind of *drive* 'trial and error':

> If a complex includes chiefly responses which happen [note 'happen'!] to be more or less appropriate to bringing about a determinate result, the complex continuing to consist of these responses until the result occurs and then shifting, the behavior of the organism would properly be designated as telic – a series of responses each of which appears as a 'trial' and each but the necessary ones as an 'error'. We may call this type of dominant complex a 'drive'.

It would seem that the crux of the behaviouristic doctrine is the idea that the consequents – either anticipated or actual – are not causal in the nexus of stimulus–response. Yet here is a type of action which does not *rest* until a *certain* consequent transpires. Is this 'satisfaction' of the drive, the attainment of the 'purpose' in pursuit of which the act is effected? How can one speak of a 'trial', much less an 'error' in behaviour without tacitly implying an end or objective? The end clearly constitutes the criterion upon which such a judgment is made by the observer *and* the determining principle of the action. In short, the 'drive' implies reaching for a consequent whose absence *causes* the act. The line of causation runs, therefore, not from precedent to consequent but from anticipated consequent to precedent, not behaviouristically but purposefully.

7 Radical Individualism: Notes on a Theory of Convergence

The theoretical discussion to this point has concentrated on the behaviouristic wing of institutionalism as expounded in Veblen, Ayres and Copeland. The balance of this book is devoted to an examination of the other, humanistic Veblen and the more humanistic wing of institutionalism exemplified by Mitchell and Commons.

But the humanistic side of the institutionalists is more apparent in their work than in their preaching. Even Mitchell, a most humanistic economist, advocated the Veblen line of efficient cause. He attacked 'the intellectualist fallacy' in economics – including his own. He declared with remarkable candour that 'Bentham cannot help toward making the social sciences valid accounts of social behavior. But better than anyone else he can help us to see the absurdity of the intellectualist fallacy we *abjure and practice*.'[1]

Because humanism was, as Mitchell said, simultaneously 'abjured and practiced', it was circumspectly swept under the methodological rug. In order to develop this side of institutionalism it is therefore necessary to construct a humanistic platform, more or less independent of the formal pronouncements of the institutionalists themselves, from which to view their own work.

Roughly at the same time as Veblen was beginning his work in social theory, the Austrian school of economics, under the leadership of the great Karl Menger, began to expand the foundations of economics into a general social theory. Names prominently associated with this development are, in addition to Menger, Friedrich von Hayek, Ludwig von Mises, Lord Robbins, Frank H. Knight and Karl R. Popper. Together they form the core of a discernible school in social philosophy which is here called 'radical individualism'.[2] It is the basic thesis of this chapter that, appearances to the contrary notwithstanding, the humanistic wing of institutionalism and the radical individualists were on a path of convergence and that, in fact, much could be gained through a merger of these apparently antipodal schools.

Radical individualism is 'radical' because it asserts that all significant human behaviour is choosing, purposive behaviour. It is individualistic because it contends that all institutions or 'social collectives' can be explained in terms of the behaviour of individuals alone.

These assertions run counter to prevailing currents of thought in psychology, anthropology, sociology and much of social philosophy. In this sense they represent a 'radical' departure from contemporary thought. But they are also 'radical' in the deeper, etymological sense of the word. They go 'back to the roots' of economics, which for over two hundred years has persistently affirmed the validity of these premises and occupied itself with developing their implications. For nearly two hundred years, too – at least from the time of the Revd Richard Jones in the first quarter of the nineteenth cetury – economics has been attacked for these premises. They have been cited as evidence of the incorrigible ignorance of the profession and they constitute a basic litany of complaint for every critic from Richard Jones through Karl Marx to the institutionalists.

The grounds of this criticism began with the nineteenth-century discovery of the cultural differences among men and the consequent rise of the doctrine of cultural relativism. It is all right to have a purposive theory of behaviour so long as men are more or less the same. But when men differ as much as they apparently do, then purposes become only the epiphenomena of human behaviour. An adequate theory must be cast in terms of those real phenomena which determine purposes. Thus, for example, Veblen, steeped in nineteenth-century anthropology and sociology, was driven by cultural relativism to reject humanism. He rejected it because, as he said, it does 'not provide a basis for the theory of the development of human nature'.[3]

This is the essential challenge to radical individualism. Cultures do, in fact, differ. Can a theory premised on purpose withstand the implications of this fact?

Whatever one may think of their solutions, the radical individualists can hardly be accused of avoiding the problems. One of their major contributions is exact specification of the two problems of institutional structure and the relativity of purpose.

Karl Menger's question, asked with regard to the institutional problem, ' "How is it possible that institutions which serve the common welfare and are the most important for its advancement can arise without a common will aiming at their creation" is still "the significant, perhaps the most significant, problem of the social sciences".'[4]

Popper observed that it is important to understand that '*only a minority of social institutions are consciously designed while the vast majority have just "grown", as the undesigned results of human actions*', and, he adds, 'social institutions may emerge as *unintended consequences* of rational actions'.[5]

Hayek said, in a similar vein, that the outstanding problem of the social sciences is to create a 'compositive theory of social phenomena' in order to 'grasp how the independent actions of many men can produce coherent wholes, persistent structures of relationships which serve important human purposes without having been designed for that end'.[6]

This is the institutional problem. The fundamental problem of purpose has never been stated better than by Frank H. Knight:

> Wants are usually treated as *the* fundamental data, the ultimate driving force in economic activity, and in a short-run view of problems this is scientifically legitimate. But in the long-run it is just as clear that wants are dependent variables, that they are largely caused and formed by economic activity. The case is somewhat like that of a river and its channel; for the time being the channel locates the river, but in the long-run it is the other way.[7]

With these cardinal problems firmly in mind, various radical individualists appropriately turned their attention to critical examination of competing doctrines. Foremost among these are pragmatism, historicism and behaviourism.

Pragmatism is the ultra-primitive idea that institutions are the deliberate creation of man, formulated and designed to serve human desires. It is this kind of naïve interpretation of the basic premises of man as a rational, choosing creature that leads one to sympathize with even the most extreme determinists in other schools. Certainly, as the above quotations show, radical individualism has no truck with this pragmatic doctrine despite the similarity of premises. Institutions have 'just grown' as 'the unintended' result of individual actions. Such important institutions as the market were not even discovered until centuries after their existence. It is indeed 'a waste of white paper' to spend much time on refutation of this primitive conception.[8]

Much more important is the doctrine of historicism, tracing back at least to early Greek philosophy and associated prominently with the names of Hegel and Marx. Karl R. Popper has devoted much of his most productive life to examination and criticism of this doctrine in its various manifestations.

The essential feature of historicism is the idea of the immutable unfolding of history. History is made not by men, except, as Marx put it, possibly in the role of a midwife, but by its own inherent impetus.

The programme of history can, as it were, be decoded and the objective of history – the state of its final resolution – determined. It is this basically Hegelian view of history that distinguished Marx's brand of 'scientific' socialism, in his own view, from what he contemptuously described as utopian socialism. His was not a programme of reform. Rather it was the prophecy of an inevitable resultant latent in the unfolding process of history itself.

Popper's criticism of this basic premise of historicism is cast in the form of a syllogism which may be paraphrased as follows:[9]

1. Knowledge influences history.
2. It is possible to predict future knowledge (otherwise it would be current knowledge).
3. Therefore it is impossible to predict history.

Popper considers this a refutation of historicism. The word is perhaps too strong, for while it is indeed a powerful argument against historicism for most people, it would be difficult to persuade a thorough historicist of its force.[10] He would not accept the major premise. Knowledge itself, he would say, is a product of the underlying historical process. Thus, while one cannot predict future knowledge, one knows, *as a matter of principle*, that this knowledge cannot be such as to disturb the underlying process and, hence, the inevitable outcome. Thus, a historicist would assume Popper's refutation away. But even if a historicist may not be persuaded by the refutation, it at least forces him to deny the most salient feature of social evolution: the impact of knowledge on human conduct. In sum, if it does not negate this philosophy, it exposes its basic 'poverty'.

Last in this fallacious triumvirate is the doctrine of behaviourism, originating in its most extreme form with the 'thoughts' of J. B. Watson[11] and culminating in its most recent version with B. F. Skinner, 'considered to be the leading behaviorist psychologist in the world':[12]

> Dr Watson designs ... to assimilate psychology to physics, chemistry, biology and physiology: to discard everything in the older psychologies 'which cannot be stated in the numerical terms of science', in terms, that is, of matter, motion and number ... behaviorism rejects therefore the concepts of consciousness, sensation, perception, will, image, and so on.[13]

The same thesis is promoted by Skinner in discussion of his most recent book, *Beyond Freedom and Dignity*:

> A science of behavior does not ... dehumanize man; it dehomunculizes him. It rejects explanations of human behavior in terms of feelings, states of mind, and mental processes, and seeks alternatives in genetic and environmental histories. It treats a person as an object, but as an object of extraordinary subtlety and complexity, and by doing so it comes to understand him in the sense in which other sciences understand their subject matters.[14]

Friedrich von Hayek has devoted much of his philosophic works to criticism of behaviourism and the spurious 'scientism' it represents. He has also published a general theory of psychology arising out of this critical work, designed to transcend, as well, the overly simplistic utilitarian psychology. Unfortunately, Hayek's powerful critical and constructive work can only be indicated here.

Hayek accuses the behaviourists of simply assuming away the central problem of psychology by basing their formulations not on the physical world of 'objects' as their 'objective' psychology pretends to do, but, rather, on the phenomenological world of 'meaning' which is ultimately and of necessity subjective.

The central problem of behaviourism is that the 'stimulus' in the nexus of stimulus and response is *not* a property of the environment *but of the agent himself.* As Hayek says, it is characteristic of the behaviourists to assume away most of the problems of psychology by basing their formulations not on the physical world of 'objects' but on the phenomenological world of 'meaning':

> . . . behaviorism thus treated the problem of mind as if it were a problem of the responses of the individual to an independently or objectively given phenomenal world; while in fact it is the existence of a phenomenal world which is different from the physical world which constitutes the main problem.[15]

The basic problem in behaviourism is that an agent *creates* his material environment through his perceptions:

> Here a new set of problems arises with which the scientist does not directly deal. Nor is it obvious that the particular methods to which he has become used would be appropriate to these problems. The question is here not how far man's picture of the external world fits the facts, but how by his actions determined by the views and concepts he possesses, man builds up another world of which the individual becomes a part. And by 'the views and concepts people hold' we do not mean merely their knowledge of external nature. We mean all they know and believe about themselves, other people, and the external world, in short everything which determines their actions, including science itself.[16]

Bertrand Russell, with characteristic aplomb, reduces the behaviouristic aim to an *absurdum*:

> What can we say, on the basis of physics itself, is that what we have hitherto called our body is really an elaborate scientific construction not corresponding to any physical reality. The modern would-be materialist thus finds himself in a curious position, for while he may with a certain degree of success reduce the activities of the mind to those of the body, he cannot explain away the fact that the body itself is merely a convenient concept invented by the mind.[17]

As noted in the introduction to Chapter 5, there can be no doubt that Veblen clearly understood this central problem in behaviourism – the problem of *perception* and *interpretation* of the stimulus. In fact, he was among the first to see it so clearly and recognize its critical force:

> The modern catchword . . . is 'response to stimulus' . . . but the
> constitution of the organism, as well as its attitude at the
> moment of impact, in great part decides what will serve as a
> stimulus, as well as what the manner and the direction of the
> response will be.[18]

The idea of the *conditioned* response is partly an attempt to
meet this criticism.[19] The agent is 'conditioned' through the
history of past responses to respond to the current physical world
in a specific manner – that is to say, to construe the infinite variety
of the physical world in such a way as to reduce it to discrete
stimuli. There is thus a two-phase operation in the nexus of stimulus and response. There exists not only the behavioural response to
material stimulus but also another operation *determining what
shall serve as a stimulus*. But then this, the 'conditioned' part of
the response, becomes methodologically indistinguishable from
what rationalists may call the 'interest' of the agent or its 'purpose'. This is readily seen by comparing hypothetical statements
by the two schools: the behaviourist might say, 'Given this conditioning and these material conditions, the following stimuli
supervene, resulting in a response of so and so'; whereas the
rationalist would say, 'Given this "purpose" and these conditions,
the following act results.' The methodological question is not the
logical rationality of the agent or his volitional abilities, but
whether it is or is not necessary to impute some selective or dis-
cretionary property to the agent, his 'state of mind', and to
include these *imputed* (and subjective!) properties in the explanation of behaviour. The answer to this, whatever one wishes to call
these properties, is inescapably in the affirmative.

One cannot refute behaviourism in this way by showing that
they have to adopt the principles and practices of the rationalists
whom they set out to replace. It is not sufficient to show simply
that the behaviourists are necessarily inconsistent with their own
methodological programme, for there is always the possibility that
they may one day discover that materialistic factor which determines what shall be materialistic. But it is possible to show how
their behaviourism leads to much confusion and lack of plain
talk in the here and now, in daily work in the social sciences.
For since it is impossible to 'observe' purposes (or whatever),
it is necessary to impute them; and the only way they can be

imputed is by the method of empathy, introspection, or whatever one wishes to call it. Yet these 'subjective' methods are
highly repugnant to the behaviourists' palates as it is their
whole object to do away with them. Thus, while behaviourists must (unavoidably) use the same methods as the rationalists,
they like to pretend that they do not, and they tend to clothe their
analysis in a vague and misleading terminology which has to them
a more 'objective' ring than that which the frankly subjective language rationalists employ. This is misleading not only to the reader
but to the analysis itself.

Thus, behaviourism is caught in its own web; with every step it
pays homage to the enemy, wishing to escape, yet finding escape
only in obscurantism. In this respect, behaviourists are more than
a little reminiscent of the last great methodological attack on the
mainstream of economics – the *Methodenstreit* – and an observation made then may easily have been spoken but yesterday: 'In
this wise the younger generation let slip, unconscious, veiled
acknowledgments [to the mainstream] . . . perhaps the more significant because unintentional.'[20]

It is here, with aid of the critical lens provided by the radical
individualists, that Veblen comes most sharply into focus. For
reasons already indicated, Veblen felt forced, through the discovery of cultural relativity, to abandon the basic concept of sufficient reason – the idea of man as a purposive, choosing individual.
He moved, therefore, towards determinism. In this ideology he had
one of two choices. He could follow Marx down the paths of historicism, but, as shown before, he knew this way was not accept-
able. 'There are no cultural laws of the kind aimed at . . .' He
could follow the newly arisen behaviourism, but he also knew, and
he was perhaps the first to know precisely why, that this was but a
specious materialism: 'The constitution of the organism . . .
decides what will serve as a stimulus.' Forced from humanism,
unable to accept either historicism or behaviourism, Veblen fled
into obscurantism; that is one of his secrets.

But Veblen never completely abandoned humanism. Indeed, it
is the burden of the remainder of this chapter to show a possible
avenue of convergence between this humanistic side of Veblen and
the development of radical individualism. But as the thesis
develops along this path, it must necessarily draw more distant
from each school. A good amount of interpretation and extra-

polation must be done, and while the present rendition may win some accord, the writer, except where directly indicated, must alone bear responsibility.

The essential point of departure for the constructive features of radical individualism is the concept of man as a reasonably rational, choosing individual with ultimate responsibility for his fate. This implies, in the first instance, recognition of what Von Mises has called 'an insurmountable *methodological dualism*' between the natural and human sciences:

> There are phenomena which cannot be analyzed and traced back to other phenomena. . . . Reason and experience show us two separate realms; the external world of physical, chemical and physiological phenomena and the internal world of thought, feeling, valuation, and purposeful action. No bridge connects – as far as we can see today – these two spheres . . . as long as we do not know how external facts – physical and physiological – produce in a human mind definitive thoughts and volitions resulting in concrete acts, we have to face an insurmountable *methodological dualism*.[21]

Robbins captures both the letter and the spirit of this dualism in the following prophetic statement (1932):

> And thus in the last analysis Economics does depend, if not for its existence, at least for its significance, on an ultimate valuation – the affirmation that rationality and ability to choose with knowledge is desirable. If irrationality, if the surrender to the blind force of external stimuli and unco-ordinated impulse at every moment is a good to be preferred above all others, then it is true that the *raison d'être* of Economics disappears. And it is the tragedy of our generation, red with fratricidal strife and betrayed almost beyond belief by those who should have been its intellectual leaders, that there have arisen those who would uphold this ultimate negation, this escape from the tragic necessities of choice which has become conscious. With all such there can be no argument. The revolt against reason is essentially a revolt against life itself. But for all those who still affirm more positive values, that branch of knowledge which, above all others, is the symbol and safeguard of rationality in social arrangements, must, in the anxious days which are to come, by

reason of this menace to that for which it stands, possess a peculiar and heightened significance.[22]

The precise methodology is that well described by Veblen as the
method of 'sufficient reason'. In order to predict a person's
behaviour, one must put oneself 'in his shoes'. One must attempt
to understand that person through empathy – in terms of his purposes, his constraints and the state of his knowledge. All such
predictions are of necessity conditional; they are conditional on
the assumption that purposes, constraints and knowledge will not
change over the period. While the methods are thus inevitably
subjective, and large-scale historical forecasts in principle impossible, neither condition means that the knowledge derived from
this methodology is other than scientific. In order for a proposition
to be scientific, it must be in principle refutable *and that is all*.
Economics, for example, the most consistently subjective of the
social sciences, is simultaneously the most refutable and commonly
acknowledged to be among the most 'scientific'.

The central theoretical problem of radical individualism is to
'explain' or 'account for' the fact of cultural relativity in a manner consistent with its premises and the methodology flowing from
these premises.

The problem can be divided into two sub-problems: (1) the fact
that institutions or forms of social organization differ between
cultures; and (2) the fact that norms, customs and, in a way, even
purposes differ between cultures. These problems are addressed in
order.

What is an 'institution'? There is hardly any word in the
English language more ambiguous and yet more indispensable
than this. The institutionalist, Walton Hamilton, offered the following description:

Institution is a verbal symbol which for want of a better
describes a cluster of social usages. It connotes a way of thought
or action of some prevalence and permanence, which is
embedded in the habits of a group or the customs of a people. In
ordinary speech it is another word for procedure, convention or
arrangement; in the language of books it is the singular of
which the mores or folkways are the plural . . . arrangements as
diverse as the money economy, classical education, the chain
store, fundamentalism and democracy are institutions.[23]

Implicit in Hamilton's description is a very basic problem. There are individuals on the one hand and institutions on the other, and nothing in between. It is no wonder that people tend to embark on either a primitive individualism or a mystical 'collectivism'. There seems to be no bridge between the two.

But Hamilton's own description provides an essential clue to the bridge. The money economy, the chain store and democracy are different kinds of things from fundamentalism, a classical education, mores or folkways. The former are patterns of interaction between people. The latter are collections of rules and beliefs.

Institutions are properly and exclusively patterns of interaction between individuals. Customs, mores, conventions, laws, morals, beliefs or norms may be collectively called *procedures*. Whatever their particular manifestation, procedures all have this trait in common: they *establish a rule of action* (as Pierce said) for an individual. To put the distinction in the most graphic terms: an institution can only exist with two or more people in interaction; a procedure can only be followed by an individual – although several individuals can, of course, follow the same procedure.

Purposes together with procedures determine individual behaviour. This is the only theory that would be required of a Robinson Crusoe society. It is obvious that Crusoe got these traits from somewhere. Part were determined by the requirements of nature. His needs for food and shelter, together with procedures necessary for attaining them, were dictated by his biological constitution and the nature of the external world. Certain other purposes and procedures may have been handed down from his parents and his pre-island associates. These more 'volitional' purposes and procedures – those over which he has a choice – would naturally be expected to change in a transformation of his environment to an island existence. Others would not. There is nothing mysterious, certainly, in Crusoe's situation, and after one got to know him, his behaviour could be predicted with a great deal of accuracy.

The same could be said of Friday so long as he remained on his part of the island. But once Friday and Crusoe meet and begin interacting, the situation becomes vastly more complicated. There are now the different purposes and procedures of each, together with the facts of their mutual interaction – their institutional structure – to comprehend. Procedures and even purposes must be chosen by each in terms of the possible effect on the other's behaviour.

To carry the metaphor one more step: Crusoe and Friday soon discover the advantages of co-operation in certain work. They formulate a common procedure specifying the mutual acts of each – 'If you do this, I shall do that' – and an institution is born. If this institution is successful, they will probably be reluctant to change it; if not, it will be changed. If it has been successful, but after some time becomes unsuccessful, they may still be reluctant to change the procedures on which it is based until they are reasonably certain of the outcome. Bitter experience has made people natural social scientists: they have learned to appreciate and fear 'unintended consequences' of social change. This is at least part of the foundation of habit and the tenacity of custom.[24]

Once one departs from the elementary yet already complicated microcosm of the Robinson Crusoe society, another powerful element enters the situation. Crusoe and Friday entered into patterns of voluntary interactions. They established voluntary institutions in the pragmatic fashion of the 'social contract'. This option is rarely given to men. Commonly they are born into an ongoing institutional structure over which they have little control, and a major feature of the environment in which they must choose their own courses of action is the institutional structure created by others whom they do not know. People are thereby forced into involuntary patterns of interaction with others. This secondary or involuntary interaction is not necessarily a product of the plan or intent of these other people, but simply the consequence of their actions, intended or otherwise.

It is easy to see how a vastly complex social structure emerges out of the accretion of these individual interactions. It is also easy to see how such a system can evolve over time as the individuals from which it is composed change their acts and their interactions. Nor does it seem incredible that the reason why people change their behaviour is because they are no longer satisfied with the results of their procedures or even of their purposes.[25]

In sum, although the infinite complexity of an institutional structure defies total comprehension, and although the individuals within such an awesome structure indeed have little power for drastic change and a well-conditioned aversion to drastic change, there is no reason to believe that such a structure is not the result of incremental acts of choice by essentially free and rational individuals. Indeed, no other interpretation seems possible and it is *known* beyond any reasonable doubt that this is the case with at least one great institutional complex – the market economy.

The question of the relativity of purposes is much more difficult. But just as there was something to be gained in distinguishing between institutions and procedures in the previous section, there is something to be gained in addressing this problem of cultural differences with respect to purposes, by distinguishing between kinds of purposes.

In introspection, with respect to one's *own* purposes, it seems apparent that they can be arranged in the order of a hierarchy, sorted in terms of comparative 'value'. It is often, indeed always, necessary to sacrifice one purpose in some degree in order to attain another. Without this problem of multiple purpose (and scarce resources), as Robbins has observed, there would be no problem of choice. Without a multiplicity of ends no problem of choice would arise: all resources would be expended on the single objective.

Many purposes are not ultimate in any sense but, rather, 'proximate' – they are purposes serving purposes. Thus the figure of Scrooge, for example, is outstanding precisely because he wished only to make money for money's sake. For this reason he is rightly regarded as neurotic, if not psychotic, and it is taken as an indication of his return to the human fold that even he, in the end, came to realize that there were other more important things in life – like a friendly Christmas dinner – that money should be used *for*.

The profit-maximizing *Homo economicus* is of course profit-maximizing only in his role as conductor of the firm. No economist has ever thought that profit was his ultimate end in life. It has always seemed too obvious to mention (though the critics of economics never tire of mentioning it) that this fellow is trying to support his family, whom he loves, that he typically would not maximize profits in an illegal or immoral way, that his pecuniary success is a means to more important objectives, such as stature in his community and the power to express his creativity.

Veblen (the humanistic Veblen) suggests that on such grounds a very important distinction may be made. He suggests no less than that there are certain basic objectives of men rooted in their characters as biological phenomena which are *universal* among all men. Then, he suggests, there are those particular purposes, variable among time and place, which men pursue as a means to attain these basic objectives.

This distinction is implicit in Veblen's discussion of the instincts. To repeat:

> When instinct enjoins little else than the end of endeavor, leaving the sequence of acts, by which the end is to be approached somewhat a matter of open alternatives, the share of reflection, discretion and deliberate adaptation will be correspondingly large. The range and diversity of habituation is also correspondingly large.

Thus, throughout Veblen's works run phrases such as 'It may be taken as a generalization grounded in the instinctive endowment of mankind' that, in this case, the instinct of workmanship (or the idle curiosity) will continue to create knowledge. What kind of knowledge it will create is, of course, 'culturally determined'. That is to say, it is determined by the current state of knowledge in the community, what parents teach their children, and by the physical and institutional circumstances of the moment. Whether the particular knowledge created is Buddhism, voodoo or modern science is literally a procedural question. What is important is this universal impetus towards understanding.

The same is true of the emulation complex. 'Everyone desires the good opinion of his fellows' – an African Hottentot or the Man in the Grey Flannel Suit. The costumes of each differ wildly, but their intended appeal is the same. In certain areas, depending on historical circumstances, good opinion is obtained by warlike exploits, or the accumulation of wealth, through piety or through political power. Detailed historical studies can discover the sources of these essentially procedural changes in a culture – as in the evolution of western society out of medievalism to the modern era. The underlying strains are the same, the fundamental values have not changed, only the way in which they are expressed and particular paths, prescribed by the social and physical environment, by which they are attained.

It is apparent that in this construction Veblen is drawing close to the position of radical individualism. In this part of his work there is a convergence in that intelligence and choice, stemming out of that methodological dualism which sets man apart from the natural world, shapes the course of human conduct. From this bridge several exciting possibilities open up. Among these are a 'theory of the development of human nature'.

As noted before, and contrary to popular supposition, economics has never regarded anyone as a single objective maximizer as in the stereotype of *Homo economicus*. If such an obsessive person ever were to exist, the one sure thing he would not be is an economic man since he would have no problem of choice. Man, in fact, and of necessity in economics, has a multiplicity of purposes all of which he attempts to satisfy in varying degrees with the necessarily limited means at his disposal. What this implies, in the context of general social theory, is that man would be *expected* to serve various purposes in varying degrees under varying circumstances. In other words, he would be expected as a matter of *rational* choice to *change his purposes* as circumstances change.

The reason is that the multiplicity of observable purposes derives from the pursuit of *value*, and they are evaluated in terms of this ultimate criterion. This value may indifferently be described as *utility*. Whatever it is called, the assumptions are: (1) that there is a schedule of value for each purpose; (2) that the value yielded declines with the degree of that purpose obtained (diminishing marginal value); and (3) that the yield of value obtainable through pursuit of a given purpose is determined not only by that purpose's own 'value schedule' but by the external constraints variable with time and place.

It is possible to demonstrate the possibility of vast cultural changes on the basis of these assumptions. One example may briefly be mentioned. The contemporary revolt from the 'quantity of life' in advanced societies and the turn towards 'quality of life' is little more than a rational reallocation on the margin between the diminishing marginal utility of 'quantity' and the increasing marginal utility of 'quality' as the amounts supplied of the former increase and the amounts of the latter decrease by the advance of the industrial economy.[26]

The above example is cited not as a 'solution' to the problem of cultural relativity, but as a means of opening a promising line of inquiry. The example shows that a rational society can undergo vast cultural changes. Thus, the *possibility* of a theory on this basis has been demonstrated. A complete theory, however, needs elaboration on three cardinal issues: (1) the existence and nature of instincts; (2) the stability and comparability of values; and (3) the tenacity of procedures – or 'habits'. Only a bare indication of these problems is possible here.

(1) *Instincts.* Certainly the revolt against instinctive psychology was well grounded. But one suspects that in this revolt the baby was thrown out with the bathwater.[27] For example, no theory of society is adequate without an account of sex in human relations, and it is equally certain that sex fits all the requirements of an instinct. It is universal among humans, it 'drives', it can be satisfied, etc. The phenomenon of sex is conclusive proof of the *existence* of instincts. It leads one to suspect that there must be other phenomena of a similar kind.

Two strong candidates are Veblen's 'idle curiosity', the drive towards understanding; and his 'emulation complex' (so described) – the need for appreciation in the eyes of another, in the ultimate case, love.

It is not necessary to an instinct that it be directly programmed (such as in the case of sex). Veblen, for example, implies that the idle curiosity is, rather, an emergent property of an active brain. It is also possible to account for such instincts in terms of evolution. A society well embedded with an 'emulation complex' would tend to be better organized and ordered than one without; it would therefore tend to survive better and selection mechanisms could be expected to work their long-run effects. With existence (sex) and selection established beyond a reasonable doubt, the search for other instincts – direct or emergent – is worth the effort.

(2) *Values.* In the conventional economic treatment all objectives are reducible to evaluation in terms of a single criterion of value. Thus, all things are comparable, and trade-offs can be established. Further, while values may differ between individuals, they are *given* to the individual. The problem is the possibility of non-homogeneity or non-comparability of values and the possibility that values may change in an individual or entire culture over time. Both problems are subject to a kind of optical illusion. Thus, in the above example, amenities may become 'incomparably' more valuable than commodities depending on quantities – with the *same* value curves. Thus, the observation problem is almost insurmountable.

This problem is closely related to the problem of changing

values, for if, as many suspect, the mind is arrayed in topological-lexicographic order, then the slightest alteration changes the 'composition' of the whole. Values could change abruptly – simply through a change in order.[28] Little is known in this area, even in the pure mathematics of such a system.

(3) *Habit*. It is with the concept of habit that the ultimate conflict between radical individualism and other social theories occurs. It is difficult to see this precisely because the concept is itself so ill-defined and ill-used. The question is not whether people typically behave in a more or less unreflecting fashion in their day-to-day behaviour – they quite obviously do. Nor is it even a question of whether their values and character and mannerisms are 'culturally conditioned', variable with the particular history of a certain people. No one denies, in other words, that, for example, children acquire certain attitudes and customs from their parents and other people *and* that these 'traditions' substantially influence the rest of their lives.

The conflict between these schools of thought centres on the *theory of change* of these 'habits' or 'traditions'. Briefly, does man ultimately choose his traditions on rational grounds or is he a prisoner of tradition?

The answer to this question determines the shape of social theories. As Veblen clearly perceived, if man is a prisoner of habit then the method of efficient cause inevitably follows. Habits can only change through exogenous forces of (ultimately) technology, natural events or wars, famines and the like. If, on the other hand, men can rationally question and choose their habits, then the theory of change reduces ultimately to the state of their knowledge – an endogenous force.

The problem once more reduces to one of the reality of freedom or the mere illusion of freedom.

Veblen chose the latter in a formulation which has since become typical in the social sciences: 'Instead of pleasure ultimately determining what human conduct shall be, the tropismatic propensities that eventuate in conduct ultimately determine what shall be pleasurable.'[29]

This phrase more than any other puts the issue squarely, and it is precisely wrong. The attitude that men are prisoners of habit developed from incorrect interpretations of fact. The fact that cultures differ was not attributed to differences in material circumstances and knowledge, as it should have been, but to the force of habit. Now that knowledge is spreading through the world and material circumstances are becoming more uniform, people are tending to converge to more commonality and showing themselves to be 'at heart' the same.[30]

Habits are a mere convenience practised for lack of a better method of conduct, highly variable with the growth of knowledge, in the end the greatest myth and obstacle to the advance of social theory.

This brief sketch may be summarized by saying that society is represented by the pattern of interaction between its individual members. These institutional structures are in turn determined by the purposes and procedures pursued and followed by these individuals. Purposes and procedures are selected in terms of their results – their 'pay-off' in the light of underlying values. These values represent certain universal characteristics of men ultimately determined by man's instinctive constitution. With such a construction men will acquire a great variety of characteristics, depending on historical circumstances. They will also exhibit many similar qualities. No theory is adequate unless it can account for these vast differences in people within a context of basic similarity.

Such a system could tend towards an equilibrium. There is an inherent conservatism in men, a propensity to habit, a reluctance to change something that works. But rarely – perhaps only in isolated island communities, if then – is anything approaching stable equilibrium attained. The sources of disturbance are omnipresent, both in the external environment and in the human brain, and any disturbance sets off a 'concatenation of cumulative sequences', as Veblen says, through the structure in a perpetual round of cultural change. Some of the central causes of change are:

(1) Exogenous forces such as pestilence, famine and war sometimes deliver fundamentally traumatic blows to a social order. One of the most dramatic examples is the Black Death of 1348 which delivered an effective *coup de grâce* to medievalism. In the economic respect alone, the wholesale decimation of people so changed the relative prices of land, labour and capital that it was no longer possible for the landed aristocracy to muster sufficient resources to maintain their power, status and security against the competing

efforts of the city merchants and the monarchy. Briefly, the feudal objectives no longer 'worked' within the new constraints and were replaced, through a process of accretion, by those of the capitalistic and nationalistic systems. This is not to mention the effects of the trauma in other dimensions, such as the wholesale discrediting of religion, the consequent spread of atheism, and attendant changes in morals and methods to the Machiavellian archetype of the Renaissance.

(2) The advancement of knowledge may itself discredit received objectives. Veblen exposed the inherent futility of conspicuous consumption. Marx advised the masses to rise since 'you have nothing to lose but your chains'. (As Veblen observed, a remarkable piece of hedonism!) Sons of successful businessmen observe their fathers' climbing the long ladder of success only to find very little at the top, and react accordingly. In one way or another the objectives of conspicuous consumption, of keeping one's place in terms of material success, fail to meet the test of serving basic values and are accordingly and rationally replaced.[31]

(3) Sometimes the very success of objectives can be their undoing. As noted before, there can be little doubt that the current substitution of leisure for work, of 'quality of life' for 'quantity of life', is a direct outcome of the affluent society. It is a straightforward allocation of the margin between competing values. The evolution of the affluent society, both in terms of cause and consequence, is one of the great cultural changes in the history of the western world. The predominant purposes have changed dramatically, but it does not represent a change in values, nor is it mysterious or surprising.

Finally, it may also be observed that because of the close interdependence between objectives in a society through status, emulation, criticism and comparative testing, a small number of people, in certain cases even perhaps a single charismatic figure, can set off cumulative sequences of changing objectives throughout the social structure. Whatever the source, however, the essential connection in the process of all social change is the individual confrontation and evaluation of procedures (including purposes) in terms of basic and, one may hazard, universal values.

APPENDIX[1]

When Veblen was writing, the intellectual world was still capti-
vated by the wonderful clockwork of Newtonian mechanics.
Everything – including man – had its place in the differential
equations of 'efficient cause'. Veblen died before the full impact
of indeterminacy in physics had time to trickle to the outside
world.[2] The great physicist Arthur Holly Compton summarized
the impact of these discoveries by saying, '. . . it is no longer justi-
fiable to use physical law as evidence against human freedom'.[3]

The rise of indeterminism in physics, while undermining the
older objections to freedom, hardly provides an entrancing alternative. The lesson, such as it is, from this development is that of
random variations – pure chance – which means, in the human
context, simply 'a higher degree of irresponsibility'.[4]

This discussion has profited before from the technique of com-
plicating, with third terms, dualisms. The temptation to search
for something between determinism and randomness is, again,
irresistible. As Popper says,

> What we need for understanding rational human behaviour
> and indeed, animal behaviour – is something *intermediate* in
> character between perfect chance and perfect determinism –
> something intermediate between perfect clouds and perfect
> clocks.[5]

There are phenomena which appear to exercise choice and
there are other phenomena which do not. While it is impossible to
know where on the continuum the distinction occurs, the poles are
well defined: man at the one extreme, say, and a stone at the
other. The task is to find another factor similarly arrayed along
this continuum; that is, some property that choosing phenomena
possess, which is not possessed by non-choosing phenomena.

An immediate candidate is a 'brain' or, more generally, a
nervous system. With the demise of anthropomorphism (which
means man-like *choosing* behaviour), the continuum of choice may
be immediately reduced to creatures with 'brains'.

But this perhaps leaves an amoeba with an Einstein,[6] which is assurance that the distinction is not yet complete. There is something more than just a 'brain' involved. The possession of a brain is a necessary, but not sufficient, condition to choice.[7]

Part of the sufficient conditions, one may suggest, is a certain kind of brain – a *simulating brain*. The human brain has the remarkable capacity to imagine alternative worlds past or future. It can generate alternative 'scenarios' and select between these scenarios in terms of their desirability (as ends) or efficiency (as means). If one is prepared to grant that at least the human mind can do this much (and a demonstration is offered immediately below), then one can deny the reality of human choice only by denying the implementation of these scenarios.

However, there are any number of everyday observable *facts* which would refute this denial (and thus tend to confirm the theory of a simulating capacity *together with* the power to act on the simulations selected).

A most striking test is in the different 'pursuit paths' of a dog and a man chasing a ball. This is shown in Fig. 1.

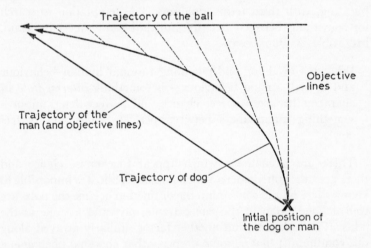

The dog aims as the *present* position of his objective – shown in the sequence of objective lines in Fig. 1. Thus, he converges through an arc on his target. The man simulates the trajectory, the (reducing) speed of the ball and his own speed, and aims at an *anticipated* point or a future state of the ball.[8]

Now a behaviourist may object that at least one form of

machine can do the same thing. A computer can also simulate future states, evaluate them, and act upon them. Thus, in the first instance of such a machine, automatic anti-aircraft guns could simulate the future state of an aeroplane, aim and fire at this future position – just like a human gunner.

But rather than a counter-argument, this example becomes a confirmation of the thesis. For the computer is considered similar to a human, apart from all other (non-cybernetic) machines, precisely because it shares this unique property.

It is of course true that the computer at present is still the slave of man in the very strict sense that the ability to choose must be given to it by a superior being in the form of its programme. And it is true that this ability to choose remains the ultimate mystery of social philosophy. Some suspect that a sufficiently complex computer would create an emergent property of self-conscious choice. However that speculation turns out, the *fact* of human choice is established beyond any reasonable doubt, and any theory of man must begin with that fact.

8 Wesley Clair Mitchell

Wesley Clair Mitchell was the second eldest of seven children, born in a small-town doctor's family in Rushville, Illinois, in August 1874. His father, Dr John Wesley Mitchell, was a doctor in the Civil War and became acquainted with Mitchell's mother through the mails as a sort of 'pen-pal'. Immediately upon the cessation of the war, after a brief stint in the hospital, Dr Mitchell rushed to Chicago and proposed to Medora Seely, his bride-to-be. She thought it would be best to wait awhile; he went away, not to return for six years! When he did return, after a marriage ending in divorce, he again proposed and she, six years the wiser, accepted. This unusual courtship was later somewhat paralleled in Wesley Mitchell's own experience. While teaching in Berkeley, California, he renewed his acquaintance with Lucy Sprague, the daughter of a wealthy Chicago wholesaler, O. S. A. Sprague, then convalescing in California. After some time of casual acquaintance, hardly a courtship, Wesley proposed by letter. She sent a letter across town gently refusing him. For four years they avoided one another. They eventually met on a hike in the mountains and, after much critical analysis of one another, agreed to marry.

Mitchell's life, from the time of his enrolment at the age of eighteen in the first class of the newly-formed University of Chicago to his death in October 1948, was marked by a serenity and personal tranquillity that only professional dedication and a good marriage can bring. He was a dedicated apostle of the creed that the scientific study of society could improve human welfare and devoted himself to the lifelong study of business cycles. His inner conviction and his professional success released him to enjoy life in its simple things: hikes, woodshop, light reading, his family and friends – curiously, never music. His was an unusually stable personality – as his doctor described him, 'the most normal man he ever knew'. Kindly, lovable, capable of inspiring the greatest affection among his colleagues, dedicated, articulate, with an immense capacity for work: altogether an outstanding individual – outstanding perhaps because of his very normalcy!

Mitchell's first year at the University of Chicago was marred by a curious incident. A doctor, wrongly diagnosing a heart murmur, informed him that he could not expect to live out the year. Mitchell simply studied as usual and when he went home for the summer – he thought to die – he told his father about the diagnosis. His father knew that the murmur was caused by an early bout with rheumatic fever and was furious about the mistaken diagnosis. He told Mitchell that 'I saw no reason for worrying you about it as I knew you were *moderate in all your ways*'. Mitchell regretted this episode because, as he told his wife, it led him to dissipation at an early age: '... he began to sit up until eleven o'clock and to drink coffee!'[1]

At Chicago, Mitchell soon established himself as a friend and colleague among the brilliant faculty there assembled. J. Laurence Laughlin, Veblen, John Dewey and Jacques Loeb, the physiologist, were among the many who were to remain friends throughout his life. Both Veblen and Dewey influenced him greatly. The only paper Mitchell preserved from these early student days indicates the close working between the various departments at Chicago, the mutual influences of Veblen and Dewey, the milieu of this brilliant early Chicago. Mitchell addressed the 'Philosophical Club' in November 1896 on the 'Austrian Theory of Value', Veblen perhaps slouching in the background, Dewey wondering if 'economic discussion had lately taken any note of biological considerations'.[2]

In 1897 Mitchell was given a travelling fellowship to Europe. He studied at Vienna and Halle, but Conrad and Menger 'made curiously little impression upon him. These men had little to contribute to the "science of economics" as Robin [his wife's pet name for him] was beginning to think of it.'[3] Mitchell returned to Chicago in 1898 and received his Ph.D. *summa cum laude* in 1899. His dissertation (later published as a part of *A History of the Greenbacks*) was indicative of his later work and preparatory to the service of what he later described to his wife as his 'vision', 'a social reorganization based on factual knowledge of how human beings behave'.[4] This vision, and the factual investigation he thought it required, occasioned perhaps Mitchell's only personal and professional conflict. He loved theory and was most at home in theory. The theoretical chapter of his *Business Cycles* was to him the most stimulating and intriguing. He nourished a lifelong ambition, never fulfilled, to write an interpretation of the development of economic theory in order to show how the theories of economists grow out of the requirements of the times in which they were formulated – his projected *Types of Economic Theory*. He also began to write at an early age *The Money Economy*, a theoretical treatment of pecuniary institutions. But first, he felt, economics must come to rest on a firmer empirical foundation, and to this goal – the improvement of the factual, empirical basis of economic science – he somewhat reluctantly devoted his life's work:

> Robin was never really trained in the technique of statistics, a fact which he always regretted. Nor did he really enjoy statistics. But social statistics seemed to him necessary if one were to make a scientific approach to the interpretation of human behavior in the economic institutions that characterize our money economy. And he thought such an interpretation of human behavior should be the basis of realistic economic theory. The new techniques in the use of social statistics which Robin developed were one of his major contributions to the science of economics. But Robin was a theorist at heart. Social statistics were not an end in themselves: they were a tool, a means to an end. Robin was a scientist by temperament and conviction, an economist by profession and became a statistician by necessity.[5]

Shortly after his graduation from Chicago, at the age of twenty-five, Mitchell worked in the Office of the Census in Washington. But he was brimming over with his own ideas and anxious to get to work on them. Consequently when Laughlin offered him an instructorship at Chicago he jumped at the chance, although he suffered an appreciable diminution of salary and had to refuse a tempting promotion in the Census. He remained at Chicago for two years and then followed Adolph Miller to the University of California at Berkeley as Assistant Professor of Commerce. The ten years at California were the years of his opus, *Business Cycles*.

Business Cycles was to be simply a part of his larger work on economic theory – *The Money Economy* mentioned above; indeed, he often speaks of it in terms of only a section of this larger work. Here again, in his letters he refers to his personal conflict between statistics and theory and, interestingly enough, what he learned by Veblen's example:

> ... You will blame me for yielding again to the temptation of figures. I used to say to myself that the *Money Economy* should not have a statistic between its covers. But that I am beginning to think a foolish idea. It is slovenly to rest content with 'very littles', 'great deal mores', and 'great importances', when even approximate precision of knowledge and statements are attainable. I want to *prove* things as nearly as may be and proof means usually an appeal to the facts – facts recorded in the best cases in statistical form. To write books of assertion, or books of shrewd observation, won't convince people who have been in the habit of asserting other things or seeing things in a different perspective. But when one can point to quantitative determinations then others must close their eyes, or accept one's results, or attack one's material, or find some new data.
>
> This feeling has been growing upon me as I have realized how slight an impression Veblen's work has made upon other economists. To me he seems straight and clear; but when others contest his conclusions I often find that the only real answer lies in doing a lot of work with statistics – work which Veblen has not performed. The fact that his works lack (in appearance far more than in reality) a basis of exact investigation further gives even a feeling that it is ingenious speculation – stimulating, but not to be reckoned with seriously. If he adduced evidence for the points susceptible of definite proof, his views upon other points would find readier credence – or at least more careful attention.[6]

Mrs Mitchell notes, 'I think the criticism he levels at Veblen, he was also levelling at his own manuscript of the *Money Economy*.'[7]

But it is apparent from these letters, as well, that as Mitchell became more involved in the *Business Cycles* his larger goal was sacrificed, to a degree, to his love of this specific problem. He writes in a charming letter regarding a proposed class on this subject:

> Will it be impossible to thrill a class of 150 freshmen with the delicate harmonies of the system of prices? Will they fail to grasp the aesthetic perfection of hair-poised adjustments

between the raging forces which push wages up and down? Will they miss that sense of impending doom hanging over the fair fabric when the stresses begin inexorably to accumulate within the system? Will the panic have no terrors for their frivolous minds, and the long-drawn liquidation – will it be a matter to sleep through? And when the wholesome readjustments have been worked out will they miss the joy of a happy ending and a fresh beginning?[8]

The above letter was written from Harvard, where he had accepted a one-year lectureship in 1908. He did not enjoy Harvard, and felt it placed too much emphasis upon classroom erudition, to the expense of research. He felt alone and stifled there and was only too glad to return to his beloved California in 1909.

Mitchell plunged into the writing of *Business Cycles* with gusto; this enormous task did not, however, prevent other activities. He wrote, on 11 December 1911, 'Today I have really been writing on Chapter XII with success. Tonight I must read to the poetry circle. Tomorrow comes my last lecture. Tuesday night a talk on Socialism in the city. Then work – hurrah!'[9]

By the time of the publication of *Business Cycles* in 1913, Mitchell had moved to New York. His classes at Columbia University and for a time at the New School for Social Research which he helped found, and his close association with high government figures in Washington, are legend. It was an ambitious and productive life, yet a singularly quiet and serene life as well. When Mitchell reached seventy years of age, he retired his position at Columbia, resigned as director of the National Bureau, seeing it over safely into the hands of Arthur F. Burns, and slipped quietly into retirement. He continued to work and write through two heart attacks, but finally the inevitable happened. He was reading some manuscripts he had written but two days before. 'Suddenly he looked up and said, "I can't understand what I have written."'[10] After a short illness he died.

Mrs Mitchell recalls Wesley telling her of one of his dreams in these last lingering weeks of his life. He dreamed that he had discovered a set of exact and precise records of the economic life in ancient Athens – where the members of families worked, how much they got, what they consumed:

The records went back to barter times. But, more than that,

the people of Athens had kept barter going continuously along with money exchange. The records showed, along with money prices, just what a bushel of wheat or a cow could be exchanged for. 'You see,' he said, 'along with all the fluctuations in the value of gold and silver we had a constant measure in terms of basic commodities.' His smile was wistful and humorous as he said, 'Too bad it was a dream. They were the sweetest records anyone could wish for.'[11]

Mitchell's concern over the psychological basis of economics and its relations to pecuniary institutions is revealed in such essays as 'The Rationality of Economic Activity', 'Bentham's Felicific Calculus', 'Postulates and Preconceptions of Economic Science' and 'The Role of Money in Economic Theory'. These essays revolve around the central problem of what Mitchell calls 'the intellectualist fallacy':

Jeremy Bentham has one service yet to perform for students of the social sciences. He can help them to work free from that misconception of human nature which he helped their predecessors to formulate. This role of emancipator he plays in the following paper.

In the social sciences we are suffering from a curious mental derangement. We have become aware that the orthodox doctrines of economics, politics, and law rest upon a tacit assumption that man's behavior is dominated by rational calculation. We have learned further that this is an assumption contrary to fact. But we find it hard to avoid the old mistake, not to speak of using the new knowledge. In our prefaces and introductory chapters some of us repudiate Hedonism and profess volitional psychology or behaviorism. Others among us assert that economics at least can have no legitimate relations with psychology in any of its warring forms. In the body of our books, however, we relapse into reasonings about behavior that apply only to creatures essentially reasonable.[12]

Ricardo was the main perpetrator of this fallacy in Mitchell's view:

. . . . while Ricardo allowed that the 'real or fancied' advantages which some employments have over others produce inequalities in both wages and profits, he at once assigned these notions the fixity of habits. The resulting inequalities thereby became constants in his problem: constants to be mentioned and then set aside. It did not occur to him that a constant required analysis. To say that some factor is fixed by habit was a happy ending of the story in Ricardo's mind. What fixed the habit and whether it remains fixed are modern questions.[13]

Mitchell notes (citing Bagehot) that Smith thought there was a 'Scotsman inside every man'.[14] Later in Ricardo's day, the idea of 'behavior as a calculating pursuit of self-interest' was 'self-evident even to the ignorant'; now, however, 'it is self-evident only to the ignorant, but they are many':[15]

The man who studies strikes and lock-outs, the shifting fortunes of business combinations, modern methods of overcoming 'consumer resistance', or business booms or depressions, does not confirm the impressions of human rationality conveyed by our theoretical treatises.[16]

Finally, Mitchell spoke of

The rediscovery of man's irrationality . . . psychologists revealed the artificiality of the Hedonistic analysis. Thinking appeared to be at best an intermittent process concerned with the humble task of finding ways toward ends set by more fundamental forces, and engaged in typically when routine modes of action encounter obstacles.[17]

Mitchell thought Veblen had pointed in the correct direction. He says that while Veblen's own conclusions are not necessarily more testable than those of the older economists, they represent a great step in the right direction – a step away from 'normal' behaviour towards 'actual' behaviour. The following citation shows Mitchell's basic attitude:

One of the ways to press forward along Veblen's path is to turn back and test for conformity to 'fact' our plausible reasonings about how men behave – that is, to see how our theories about what men do agree with what we can observe. Of course, what we can observe is not wholly objective. As recalled above, it depends upon what we are mentally prepared to see, and also upon our techniques. Yet when we can apply them, factual tests of ideas are one of our most effective ways of promoting knowledge. The men who laid the foundations of economics recognized this point, and in their writings upon method admitted the desirability of 'inductive verification'. But in practice they spent little effort upon this desideratum – it seemed too hopeless a task as matters stood. The notion that inquiries *should be framed from the start* in such a way as to permit testing the hypothetical conclusions was not common property in their time. Unless such plans are laid in advance, and laid with skill, it is more than likely that the results attained by reasoning will be in such form that no inquirer can either confirm or refute them by an appeal to fact. Observing this run of affairs, the classical methodologists spoke disparagingly of induction in general and of statistical induction in particular. It seemed to them a tool limited to a narrow range of uses in economics. Veblen's case is not so very different, except that he deals with '*actual*' as distinguished from '*normal*' behavior. He does not plan in advance for testing his conclusions.[18]

This distinction between the 'actual' or the 'statistically average', as he sometimes called it, and the 'normal' behaviour examined by economists was very influential in Mitchell's thinking. Basically it reduces to a rejection of the model-building, equilibrium-tending, rationalistic formulations of orthodox economics. In searching for an example of this normalizing attitude in received economics, Mitchell discovered a striking citation from Ricardo. Mitchell said:

Our economic theory is less an account of what men actually do than a statement of what as rational for them to do, as seen by a shrewd fellow citizen. Ricardo expressed this difference clearly in the remarkable letter to Malthus written Oct. 22, 1811, concerning international shipments of money. 'I assume,' he says, 'that nations ... are so alive to their advantage and profit ... that in point of fact money never does move but when it is advantageous ... that it should do so. The first point to be considered is, what is the interest of countries in the case supposed? The second, what is their practice? Now it is obvious that I need not be greatly solicitous about this latter point; it is sufficient for my purpose if I can demonstrate that the interest of the public is as I have stated it. It would be no answer to me to say that men were ignorant of the best and

cheapest mode of conducting their business . . . because that
is a question of fact not of science and might be urged against
almost every proposition in Political Economy.'[19]

It is apparent that what Mitchell discussed here is fairly and
insightfully stated. He has, in fact, encountered the rough dimensions of the 'fundamental methodological dualism' between the
method of the physical and the social sciences discussed before.
Further, it is true that the conclusions of economics, at least the
important conclusions, are not as amenable to empirical test as
those of the physical sciences. In the terminology current at the
time (and which later caused a great deal of confusion as shown
below), the important conclusions of economics are 'deduced'
from underlying premises; they do not relate to inductively
established empirical generalizations. Thus, Mitchell's concern
over the psychological foundations of economics was derived
from a deeper concern over its methodology. He felt, in a word,
that a rationalistic approach did not yield testable conclusions.
Therefore, he was concerned over the scientific legitimacy of
economics. This methodological concern and the way in which it
was expressed caused a small revival of controversy reminiscent
of the *Methodenstreit* of several decades before.

One of the securest opinions about institutionalism, especially
held by the opponents of institutionalism, is that it surely lies in
close and intimate relation to the school of *Historismus*. One
aspect of this opinion, the idea that Veblen is Hegelian in a significant way, has already been examined. The other aspect of the
same opinion, that Mitchell is inductivist in a significant way, is
the concern of this small section.

As noted in the Introduction, the years preceding the rise of
institutionalism were years significantly marked by the great
Methodenstreit between the German historical school and
Menger, Böhm-Bawerk and others. This controversy carried
over, like shadows in the cave, to the American scene with the
abrupt rise and fall of the American historical school. Consequently, economists at the turn of the century, having either
directly or vicariously gone through two or three decades of
internecine warfare, were cocked and primed – on their theoretical hackles as it were – against any taint of *Historismus*. Veblen's
historical 'stages' made them uneasy and suspicious; but when

Mitchell came out with his statistically detailed work, the inductive cat which they thought safely bagged and sunk to the bottom of the river seemed once more to have slipped out of the deductive bag.

If the first American *Methodenstreit* over the historical method was but a pale reflection of its German counterpart, the second was surely a parody. An opposition too eager to polish up a fine armoury of rusting dialectical weapons; an uneasy and confused defence not too sure what the whole thing was about. The theoretical Agincourt arrived when Mitchell realized he had a couple of concepts – really just words – mixed up, and the second American *Methodenstreit* collapsed around 1930.

But to say that this was not a significant controversy in methodology does not mean that it was not significant to the history of institutionalism. For it caused no end of obfuscation of the real issues between institutionalism and other schools, not only then, but even now.

The controversy started – ironically enough from what is now known of Mitchell's own theoretical tastes and his own view of the *Business Cycles* – with the publication of this heavily statistical work. The first sizzling blast came, predictably, from Germany in a review by Dr Adolph Löwe. Löwe said, '. . . it is theory which provides the principles by which the irreproducible fullness of reality can be set in order; it is theory which formulates the questions which the facts must answer'.[20] Mitchell replied that this is quite obviously true, if a little 'schematic':

> Dr Löwe's view of the relations between fact and theory in scientific work is a common one. But it seems to me over-schematic. Against the statement, 'one cannot set economic facts in order unless one has a theory' (I should prefer to say 'hypothesis'), can be put the statement, 'one cannot form an economic theory unless one knows some facts'. And both these statements overlook the fact that the two categories are not mutually exclusive. The theories with which science works cannot be conceived as existing apart from the facts of human experience, and men can apprehend facts only in terms of notions with which their minds are furnished. The more thoughtfully one considers the relations between these two phases of knowing, the less separable they become.[21]

The controversy over the methodological implications of the *Business Cycles* dragged on intermittently for some years and finally reached its head in a meeting of the American Economic Association in 1925.

Mitchell was then president of the American Economic Association. He chose for his presidential address the subject 'Quantitative Analysis in Economic Theory'. He wished to make essentially two points: (1) to voice his dissent to the proposition that the only function of 'quantitative methods' and/or statistics is to provide factual tests for the received hypotheses and doctrines of economics; and (2) to express his concern with the method of economic inquiry as traditionally followed in classical and neo-classical work. As to this latter point, the programme he outlined is decidedly in favour of piecemeal induction at the expense of general, systematic theories.

In reaction to Marshall's famous opinion that qualitative analysis cannot proceed much further, and that the further growth of economic understanding 'must wait upon the slow growth of more realistic studies', Mitchell said, 'Quantitative analysis shows no more promise of producing a statistical complement to pure theory than it showed when Dr Marshall pronounced his dicta.'[22] The reasons for this, he clearly indicated, are the 'normal' as opposed to the 'actual' character of economic propositions. Having proceeded this far, Mitchell clearly wavered between two possible conclusions: he could either advocate retaining the method of traditional economics and reformulating its propositions in a way amenable to statistical attack; or he could advocate junking both the method and the content of received economics and proceed on a methodological line suggested by the new quantitative analysis.

He strongly suggested the former, as, for example, when he recognized the need for qualitative work:

> ... I shall say little of qualitative analysis beyond making the obvious remark that it cannot be dispensed with, if for no other reason, because quantitative work itself involves distinctions of kind, and distinctions of kind start with distinctions of quality.[23]

He also restricted himself to the recognition that quantitative methods imposed only certain 'technical constraints' on the theorist:

> ... in preparing for their work, the quantitative theorists usually find it necessary to formulate problems in a way different from that adopted by qualitative theorists; this technical necessity of restating problems promises to bring about radical changes in economic theory.[24]

But this moderate position rapidly shaded off to the radical side in Mitchell's 'address' and ended in one startling paragraph which, as Schumpeter remarks, describes 'even to details, the position which Schmoller held throughout his life'.[25]

> ... I do not mean that we can expect the rapid crystallization of a new system of economic theory built by quantitative analysis. Quite the contrary, the literature which the quantitative workers are due to produce will be characterized not by general treatises, but by numberless papers and monographs. Knowledge will grow by accretion ... [as] it grows in the natural sciences, rather than by excogitation of new systems. ... It will be harder for anyone to cover the whole field, perhaps quite impossible. From time to time someone will try to give a comprehensive survey of the results of quantitative research, but such books will not have the prestige won by the treatises by Adam Smith, Ricardo, Mill and Marshall.[26]

Historismus incarnate! Prescribed by a great institutionalist and doubtless the major source of that inductivist taint with which institutionalism has since become associated.

One cannot deny that in Mitchell's 1925 'address' there exists clear and unambiguous evidence to the support of the historico-inductivist interpretation, but it must be realized that this evidence remains valid for at most three years. It was specifically denied by Mitchell in 1928.

The occasion for Mitchell's methodological about-face was a 'Round Table Discussion' between himself, Jacob Viner and others on 'The Present Status and Future Prospects of Quantitative Economics'. Viner became the protagonist with a very tart criticism of inductivism and, by implication, of Mitchell and his 1925 'address'. Viner began with a concession to quantitative analysis. 'It seems to be true,' he says,

as we are told so often by the exponents of the quantitative
method in economics, and as we could not have well avoided
knowing even if they had not spoken on the subject, that in the
physical sciences progress has consisted in the discovery of
quantitative differences underlying what first appeared to be
solely differences in kind. . . .[27]

'No one', he observed, would question that 'in one direction at
least the path of progress in economics will approximate the
direction which the physical sciences have taken. That this calls
for great investigations of the statistical type, and is largely
dependent upon the elaboration and development of more precise
statistical tools, goes without saying', he continued. The precise
nature of the contribution that quantitative economics will be
able to make in this direction is a matter of conjecture, but it
may well be of the nature of 'laws in statistical form summarizing
the observed mass behavior of mankind in the world of price
phenomena'. 'This,' he said, 'sounds like an important concession to the possibilities of quantitative analysis in economics, and
so it is intended.'[28]

Viner next, in oblique reference to Mitchell's 'address', turned
to the belief that the trend of future economics is inductive.
Such a view, he said, stems from a confused identification
between 'quantitative analysis' and the mere 'accumulation of
statistics'. With this identification he in no way agreed and
wished it to be made crystal-clear that his 'concession' in no way
conceded to this view:

> There is an important distinction between statistical classifica-
> tion, compilation, on the one hand and economic analysis on
> the other. Economic theory and political arithmetic are not
> the same thing any more than barometric readings and meteor-
> ology are the same thing.[29]

Statistics must necessarily, inevitably, remain simply a tool of
theory. It 'is the *sole task* of economic *theory*' to 'search for
mutual dependencies, for covariation', and

> index numbers, estimates of national income and so forth, no
> matter how much genius and theory may have gone into
> their attainment, once achieved are by themselves merely edi-
> fying facts and serve no imaginable purpose except as the

theorist uses them as means to the discovery of relationships between things.[30]

Lastly, so as to leave no doubt as to the particular persons and programmes to which this indictment was addressed, Viner called up a past example of the effects of such a programme as Mitchell seemed to advocate:

> Several years ago there was a sudden wave of enthusiasm among American pedagogues for the Pearsonian coefficient of correlation, and a plague of graduate students in education spread itself over the land and began correlating furiously and indiscriminately and with an inverse correlation between zeal and discretion which seems closely to have approached, if not quite to have attained, perfection . . . there are ominous signs . . . that economics is becoming similarly infected.[31]

The new programme in economics, he concluded, are 'almost precisely identical' to this past pedagogical situation and 'to the prophecies of the German historical school some sixty years ago, and *it is this resemblance alone which causes me concern*'.[32]

Mitchell's retort to Viner's strictures simply assumed the form of an unqualified assent. He wondered not at the validity of Viner's position, but that Viner should bother to mention the thing at all! He seemed to have completely forgotten his 1925 methodological position:

> I know no competent economist who would subscribe to the one-sided views which have been imputed this morning to persons unnamed. On the contrary, *I agree that the man-of-straw merits the fate for which he has been set up*. And if anyone should suggest that my notions about the service which quantitative analysis may render to economics are those of the straw man, I should still see no ground for controversy. All I need to do in that contingency is to ask the critic to read what I have said before on this topic.[33]

An interesting postscript to this discussion appears by way of John D. Black's comments, subsequent to the statements by Viner and Mitchell, Black was properly astonished at Mitchell's new position and declared that Mitchell could 'render no greater service' to 'the cause . . . than to rewrite his presidential address in such a way as to leave out a number of equivocal statements'.[34] Mitchell never did this, but in compiling the series of essays, *The Backward Art of Spending Money*, Joseph Dorfman appropriately included Mitchell's 1928 statement as an appendix to his 1925 presidential address,[35] providing thereby a much-needed correction of the record.

If one were to plot Mitchell's 'theoretical' or 'deductive' stance on a graph, it would appear very high on the vertical scale in 1914, at the time of the first edition of the *Business Cycles*; then perhaps a progressive decline to the bottom of the trough in 1925; a rapid recovery by the second edition of *Business Cycles* in 1927, attaining its initial high in 1928; and thence, a secular incline through subsequent years. By 1934, for example, Mitchell could laugh with his students at 'what seems to us now the rather stupid program of the historical school proper, simply to collect materials over two or three generations and see what they could establish'.[36]

A reviewer of this episode in economic history would naturally be led to look for some great trauma, some devastating critique, to Mitchell between these years 1925 and 1928. He would naturally inquire as to what happened to Mitchell to revolutionize so completely his methodological position through these three years so that by the latter date he could not even understand what all the fuss was about. The answer is that nothing happened. Nothing, that is, except that Mitchell realized one simple fact which he had temporarily forgotten. This fact is that he could, if he wished, scrap the whole of received economic doctrine – its theorems and systems, its assumptions and even the 'intellectualist fallacy' – without touching the inductive–deductive controversy at all. Once he clearly realized this fact, Viner's strictures seemed remote, as indeed they were. Thus one finds, in a brief discussion in 1927, Mitchell commenting on the fact that it is a 'blunder to identify quantitative method with induction and the process by which orthodox economic theory was developed with deduction'.[37] Once he realized this, his assent to Viner's strictures followed as a matter of course.

The clue to both Mitchell's methodological oscillations and to the methodological reception of institutionalism by those of the mainstream followed the basic form of a *non sequitur*: (a) received theory is deductive; (b) institutionalism rejects received theory; therefore (c) institutionalism is non-deductive (and hence inductive).

Mitchell had a 'vision' – 'the alluring possibility of shaping the evolution of economic life to fit the developing purposes of our race ... of which we catch fleeting glimpses in our more sanguine moments!'[38] This vision led him both to his institutionalism and to his emphasis on factual data. Economics was not a mere plaything to Mitchell; it was something that could do good. But this meant something that had to pertain to reality, to the practical life of everyday economic intercourse. In his words, in order to do good it had to reach a state where the 'theoretical part' and the 'applied part' of economics textbooks would be united by something 'more intimate than the binding'.[39] In casting about for reasons for the apparent failure of received economic theory to apply to the problems of the world, Mitchell found the fault to lie in the normalized case which resulted from certain deductions about what was rational for men to do, given certain circumstances and motives. What they ought to do, he felt, is not what they do do, and the concern over the former led to the neglect of the latter, to the expense of applicability. Thus, he wished to change the way of arriving at behavioural hypotheses in economics: 'Instead of starting with a set of motives and showing how human beings thus constituted may be expected to act, he (the economist) can inquire (statistically) *how actual men conduct themselves.*'[40]

This, he felt, certainly did not involve approaching the 'facts' with a 'clean slate', or the rejection of theory or deductive methods; on the contrary, what he wished for was a general theory whose behavioural hypotheses were 'framed from the start' to allow for statistical test. This kind of theory he thought he found in Veblen. Veblen was not in the least concerned with how men ought to act or how it was in their best interests to act; rather he was content to describe how (in his eyes) they do act in given circumstances – even, as it may be, against their own best interests. This, Mitchell decided, was a more realistic approach than the older method:

... to find the basis of economic rationality in the development of a social institution directs our attention away from that dark subjective realm, where so many economists have groped to an objective realm, where behavior can be studied in the light of common day.[41]

In conclusion, one cannot but feel that Mitchell was only a few years ahead of his time in the sense that, were he working today, he would feel quite comfortable in the mainstream of economics. Certainly the rise of econometrics would please him, although he may share with many economists today a certain dismay over its statistical pretensions as compared to its quantitative significance. Perhaps even more, recent work in welfare economics and attempts to integrate economic and political theory would have pleased Mitchell. Under the rubric of 'market failure', welfare theory has greatly expanded knowledge regarding the structure and functioning, as well as the limitations, of 'pecuniary institutions'.

Mitchell had a deep appreciation for the importance of the problems Veblen struggled with, but unlike Veblen and unlike most of the other institutionalists, he realized that the traditional methods of economics do not automatically preclude intelligent study of these problems. By insisting on the importance of Veblen's problems, yet refusing to lead a *Methodenstreit*, Mitchell began an important bridge between institutional and mainstream economics.

9 John Rogers Commons

John R. Commons was born in a small town in Ohio in 1862, and died in 1945. The eighty-odd years of this life span a singularly tumultuous and varied career appropriately set forth in his beautiful autobiography, *Myself*.[1]

Commons' parents left their original farm in the South and moved to Ohio, and later to Indiana, to escape the oppressive milieu of slavery. His mother was the 'strictest of Presbyterian Puritans' and named her eldest son after the martyred victim of Bloody Mary. She, a Calvinist, a leader of the 'women's' crusade against the saloon, intensely practical, was the main financial stay of the family. His father was a Darwinian, a Spencerian, a visionary and a type *par excellence* of the 'Yankee trader'. He swapped newspapers for farms, horses for harness shops, and harness shops back for newspapers. As Commons said, he 'might have given him an historical justification. He was a survival from . . . the Barter stage of economic evolution. He could not fit into the Money and Credit economy.' All in all it was an uphill financial pull when the family decided to send their son to Oberlin College in search of a career.

Commons' academic record at Oberlin was singularly undistinguished. It took him six years to complete the usual four-year course – owing in part to a 'nervous breakdown' after a Greek examination, and mostly to a curious doggedness that marked Commons' life. He seemed to grasp upon one element or thing in his classes and study it, worry it, as a dog with a bone, refusing to give up until either it or himself was ultimately defeated – to the complete neglect of anything else that might come along in the class presentations. Thus, his class in Greek was destroyed because he decided upon 'hunting up everything I could find on the letter Omega'. Biology was a loss, 'because I persisted in finding the heartbeat of a little red water-bug that came to life before the ice was out, in the roadside ditches. The other students went on with the regular schedule of specimens but I stuck stubbornly to that little bug.' Finally, in 1888, he graduated with 'poor' examination marks, but none of the professors would stand in his way.

The course of his subsequent career was more or less anticipated by a short episode of teaching after graduation from high school. He taught for a while in a small country school and decided to give his students a picture of life as it really is. The lessons were an abysmal failure:

> In passing the country slaughterhouse ... I would get the butcher to give me an ox's heart, or eye, or some other piece of anatomy, to demonstrate to the pupils the picture found in our textbook. But we never could identify a single valve or layer of muscle or anything else which we found so plainly pictured in the book. The pupils lost faith in me, tumbled me in the grass, pelted me with snowballs, and I had to resign in three months.

Following this account, Commons furnishes a telling insight into the personal make-up of the very quizzical and heretic scholar he was to become in later years. Seeing is very profoundly believing, and vice versa; the subject is only what one has found on one's own investigations into the facts. The presumption is to fact rather than to theory, to investigation rather than authority, to one's own observations, when contrary to the investigations of others. Thus, Commons explains the amusing episode above as a failure of the physiologist who wrote the text. The students 'wanted something ... for sure, handed down by the great authorities of the past, and I couldn't produce it. I vowed that never again would I teach.' This, though there is danger of making too much of it, is surely a hardy iconoclasm. When one can deny or doubt the presence of valves and muscles because one cannot find them, what infinite possibilities lay in the esoteric realm of economics!

After a brief stint in practical life, Commons decided to go to Johns Hopkins to study under Ely. Two Oberlin trustees lent him money sufficient for two years' graduate study and off he went, 'resolved to abandon all the theories of political economy which I had ever picked up, and to start, as John Locke would say, with a sheet of white paper. Within a year and a half came my usual fate.' He failed and never obtained a degree. But in this period at Johns Hopkins he succeeded in winning the friendship and respect of Richard T. Ely, and helped Ely on the draft of his *Introduction to Political Economy*. Ely sent Commons out on many case studies into building and loan societies, unions, strikes and lock-outs, and once assigned him the task of obtaining a pension for an old Civil War veteran. 'I visited the Pension Office, interviewed lawyers, attached myself to the Democratic Congressman from Baltimore... I got the pension. Was this political economy?' Commons implies that it was.

After Johns Hopkins, Commons experienced a series of disastrous academic failures culminating in a meteoric rise through three universities from a $1,000-a-year instructor at Wesleyan, where he was fired before the term was up, to a $1,200-a-year associate professor at Oberlin, and thence to Indiana as a $2,000-a-year full professor – all in less than two years! In 1895 an offer came from Syracuse University for a position at slightly higher pay. Commons thought he might use this offer to bargain an increase in salary at Indiana, so he told President Swain of the Syracuse offer. 'Evidently he was loaded, for he immediately pulled the trigger: "Accept the offer at once." I didn't want to accept it and did not want to leave Indiana. But now I had to leave. Never since have I asked for an increase in salary. The exposure is too dangerous.' In 1899 Commons found that his chair in sociology at Syracuse had been dissolved – largely because of his supposed 'socialist' leanings – and he found himself once again out in the world in search of a job.

Thus began five years as a freelance economist, statistician and investigator for various organizations and pressure groups. For a while he worked for George Shibley, a self-made man of wealth and part-time economist of bimetallist leanings. Commons and a collaborator were employed by Shibley to compile a weekly index of the movement of wholesale prices – the first in the country. They worked on this index for about a year and started publishing their first indexes in newspapers in July 1900. Meanwhile, Shibley had become an economic adviser to the Democratic National Campaign committee, pushing William Jennings Bryan's bimetallist policies. Again Commons' fate knocked on the door as he relates in this amusing account:

Our index number ... showed each week an average fall in prices on the gold standard, which was quite convincing for George, Bryan and the Democrats. ... But, strangely, beginning about the middle of August, the index number stopped falling. It was exactly the same as it had been the previous week. George wired me that something was wrong, and asked me to go over the figures again. ... The figures were correct. This happened again the next week. ... Stone and I issued it with anxiety. George wired again. Then, the first week of September, 1900, that blamed index number, to our consternation, began to rise. We needed to wait for the lightning only twenty-four hours. George wired, cancelling my contract ... advising me that it was my duty to find other work. ...

Commons then found employment compiling a report on immigration. He toured the country with an interpreter he found in Hull House and stayed mostly in cheap hotels and doss-houses to meet his subjects. Upon completion of his report he made the acquaintance of a commissioner on the United States Industrial Commission – the famous inquiry into trusts, high finance and capitalism, which Veblen used in his *Theory of Business Enterprise*. H. W. Phillips was the representative from Western Pennsylvania, a self-made millionaire, and determined to write a scathing minority report on the operations of big business. He hired Commons to help him. Here Commons learned

of a split in the ranks of Capitalism. It was the difference between billionaires and millionaires. Phillips was several times a millionaire, but he might have been a billionaire had it not been for John D. Rockefeller. ... I never could get my attack on the Standard Oil radical enough to suit Phillips. He was always mumbling. So one night I let loose and presented him with something that tore into the very foundations of capitalism. He recovered. My stuff was too stiff. Thereafter I thought I had his measure, and I trimmed my manuscript to fit it.

During his two-week association with Phillips, Commons was introduced to the good life. Their economic discussions were over dinner, punctuated by the pop of champagne corks:

Oh! My! Ain't it grand! Never before nor since have I known anything like it. Also we had fifty-cent cigars, moose meat, lobsters and other inspiring delicacies of the rich, I understood that Rockefeller was very abstemious, living on crackers and milk – which was a shame, considering what he might have consumed for the benefit of the poor. But not so with Phillips and me. We furnished employment for thousands, around the wide world. I think that during that period I ate only one meal a day, but took on loads of coffee to counteract the bellyful of high life.

In 1904, at the age of forty-two, Commons was called to the University of Wisconsin, largely through the efforts of his patron, Ely, and there found the security essential to the pursuit of his life's work. But even here he fell into no narrowly academic routines. He became a power in the state through his influence on the reforming Governor and later Senator, Robert M. La Follette. His teaching was constantly interrupted by the call to public service and he became a nationally recognized authority and pioneer in the problems of municipalities, labour–management relations, civil legislation, the creation and management of public utilities; he was a friend and trusted confidant of business and labour alike and a popular arbitrator of their disputes.

Here too, at Wisconsin, he found the pedagogical methods that so endeared him to his students, and to whose value they testify. His classrooms became a basis of operations, both for himself and for his students, for excursions out into the real world. In the classroom he and his students would summarize and analyse their findings. In the dedication of his autobiography, Commons explains his method of teaching in the course of reflecting upon the great friendship and love of his former students:

I have tried to analyze the friendship of my Friday Niters. I trace it back to thirty years to the time when I came to Wisconsin and had given up my first ideas of teaching. I began simply to tell my classes personal stories of my mistakes, doubts and explorations, just as they happened to occur to me, injecting my generalizations, comparisons and all kinds of social philosophies. . . . I think my students were more interested in my telling these stories and my dubious interpretations than they were when I attempted to expound systematically the consistent theories of economics. I was always casting doubt on the latter and getting my students mixed up.

That he had many and interesting stories to tell of the world
of affairs there can be no doubt. Probably no other member of
the university faculties in the United States at the time had a
comparable background and influence. Selig Perlman, his friend,
former student and colleague, briefly summarizes the more outstanding among the many practical experiences of Commons. He
worked in

> President McKinley's Industrial Commission, the Wisconsin
> Industrial Commission (1911–1913) and the United States
> Commission on Industrial Relations (1913–1916). In 1923
> with Professors Ripley and Fetter he represented four Western
> States before the Federal Trade Commission on the Pittsburg
> plus case. . . . He organized and directed the Bureau of Eco-
> nomy and Efficiency of the city of Milwaukee during the first
> socialist administration, 1910–1912.
>
> His connections with unofficial bodies were equally varied.
> Early in the century he promoted agreements between
> employers and unions for the National Civic Federation. In
> 1906 and 1907 he also investigated for the same organization
> municipal and private corporation of public utilities. In the
> same years he investigated with others labor conditions in the
> steel industry in Pittsburg for the Russell Sage Foundation.
> The American Association for labor legislation began opera-
> tions in 1909 in a corner of his university office at Madison.
> . . . He was president of the American Economic Association
> (1917), associate director of the National Bureau of Economic
> Research (1920–1928), President of the National Monetary
> Association (1922–1923), and President of the National Con-
> sumer's League (1923–1935).[2]

This is not to mention his almost constant employment as consul-
tant and political legman for La Follette in Wisconsin.

Commons enjoyed about ten years of semi-retirement and
writing in trailer camps in Florida and in the homes of friends,
before he died in 1945.

The great part of Commons' life was spent as a conscientious,
knowledgeable investigator of practical problems, and the results
of this part of his life stand in the constitutions of unions, and in
the inspired work of his students – as much a permanent monu-
ment to his memory and influence, perhaps more, than his formal

treatises and publications. With the exception of his first tentative
explorations of marginal utility theory early in the 1890s, the
great bulk of his formal publications were devoted to historical
and statistical investigations of no direct interest here. It was only
late in his life – as a sort of 'summing up' – that Commons again
turned his attention to general problems; and an exposition such
as this, by concentrating really upon the minor portion of his life,
lies in danger of neglecting what is perhaps the major part of his
work. A complete bibliography of the prodigious amount of published material under Commons' name is included as an appendix
to his last book, *The Economics of Collective Action*. Therefore
the present exposition may mention only the more outstanding
among this list.

In 1893 Commons published his one attempt at economic
theory, *The Distribution of Wealth*. It is a very curious and
almost indescribable mixture of marginal utility analysis and
something between socialism and goodwill. The book received
very poor reception in economic circles: Taussig rejected a
request to review it, saying it was an 'unbaked performance'.
From this date to his settlement at Wisconsin in 1904, Commons'
writings consisted largely of essays and articles in the various
journals, newspapers and governmental reports such as that of
the Industrial Commission on Immigration and Education in
1901, the 'Final Report' of this Commission in 1902, and the
'Report on Regulation and Restriction of Output' in 1904. In
1910 Commons (and others) published *A Documentary History
of American Industrial Society*, a massive work encompassing
some ten weighty volumes of history: 1913 to 1918 witnessed his
work on unions and labour problems, *Labor and Administration*;
in 1916 he and J. B. Andrews published *Principles of Labor
Legislation*; and in 1918 the four-volume *History of Labor in the
United States*. In 1919 he published his programmes for reform
and better labour–management relations under the title
Industrial Goodwill.

In 1924 Commons turned his attention to more theoretical
concerns with the publication of what, in the present opinion, is
his best general account of his 'theory', *The Legal Foundations of
Capitalism*. This was followed ten years later with a more precise
statement in his *Institutional Economics*; and in 1950 the post-
humous publication of the theoretical 'capstone' to his life's

work, *The Economics of Collective Action*. There is no substantial difference in the theories presented in these three works except, perhaps, that as the last two works become more precise and stratified, they neglect much of the suggestive promise of the earlier *Legal Foundations*. An idea of his prodigious output may be obtained through perusal of his complete bibliography, which comprises some twenty-five pages of small type and single-spaced reference.

Theory was never Commons' métier. What he calls his 'theories' are almost exclusively poorly wrought and somewhat lackadaisical classifications and sub-classifications of phenomena as they appear to him from a dimly-held and mainly intuitive conception impossible to define. His three 'theoretical' works present mainly a collection of *obiter dicta*, staggering, more or less randomly, between the trite and the ridiculous with many profound insights between. Thus, the prefatory cautions voiced by Commons and his admirers to any about to embark on his study, are not to be taken merely as modest euphemisms but in deadly earnest – on penalty of vast bewilderment. As Commons says:

> The comments and criticism by readers and students of both my *Legal Foundations of Capitalism* and the various mimeographical copies and revisions of this book on Institutional Economics, to the effect that they could not understand my theories nor what I was driving at, and that my theories were so personal to myself that perhaps nobody could understand them leads me to set aside personal inhibitions and boldly to treat myself as an objective Ego, participating, for fifty years, in many forms of collective action.[3]

Kenneth H. Parsons, Commons' friend, admirer and editor, observes with admirable understatement that

> His general theories are elaborations and generalizations of particular insights: he integrates his ideas around positions on the fundamental issues in social thought. This approach, this method of working out a theory of economics, may seem bewildering to persons who are schooled only in the techniques of logical exposition from assumed premises.[4]

Commons' method is, in his own words, the 'comparative method' of the investigators as opposed to the deductive methods of other economists. It consists in the search for 'similarities and differences' in the 'thousands of special cases which we are called upon to investigate'.[5] Expositionally, it is what may be termed the autobiographical method, consisting of the elucidation of a particular insight given by a personal experience in the course of interviews, travels, informal discussions or specific investigations, and generalizing these insights to cover as many cases as possible. Thus, even Commons' most theoretical works follow the expositional form: experience; insight; generalization of the insight; and lastly, other similar experiences. As to the bearing of this method upon the inductive–deductive controversy, or where it places him in the *Methodenstreit*, Commons, in effect, admits that he does not know, nor does he much care. Thus with respect to 'the economists' controversy of fifty years ago over the "deductive" and the "inductive" methods of investigation', he finds that 'the older controversies about deduction and induction disappear in the great movement to obtain Insight and Understanding'. 'Insight' is then defined as 'Illumination, Understanding, and an Emotional Sense of the fitness of things'.[6]

Commons' point of view and the object of his analysis follow as surely from his biography as does his methodology. The first sentence of the text of his *Institutional Economics* explicates his general approach: 'My point of view is based on my participation in collective activities, from which I here derive a theory of the part played by collective action in control of individual action.'[7] It is then a theory of collective action and the place of this theory in a general theory of economics:

> The problem now is not to create a different kind of economics – 'institutional' economics – divorced from preceding schools, but how to give collective action, in all its varieties, its due place in economic theory.[8]

Commons, like Veblen, wished to hang economic theory from the hooks of a general theory of social change. But he represents the very antithesis of Veblen in the substance of his theory. In Commons' theory, all social phenomena are (apparently) the product of rational decisions. Institutions, in Veblen's terminology – 'going concerns' in Commons' – are the product of rational decisions and are perpetrated and maintained in the service of a specific end.

This is the single most important thing to understand about Commons' analysis. It is particularly important for those in the Veblenian tradition to understand. For Veblen begins where Commons leaves off, and Commons nowhere indicates the slightest cognizance of Veblen's central problem. To Commons, 'institutions' are *administrative devices*, manned by 'officials', created and moulded to the service of a given objective. They are collective bodies willingly entered into for the accomplishment of things the individual cannot accomplish otherwise. They are the things that Commons worked in and helped to build throughout his life – administrative bodies of the state, unions, firms, public utilities, governed by laws and by-laws, and administered by officials. Once the fact is appreciated that such things as these are the concern of Commons' institutional economics – the single and sole object of analysis – his theory follows by easy consequence. If anything else is imputed to Commons' analysis, particularly if one attempts to impute to it any but the most remote bearing upon Veblen's kind of problem, the problem of the unintended consequences of human behaviour, the theory appears meaningless and irrelevant – as it is indeed to these problems. His is a theory of the design and administration of organizations – of 'going concerns'. Properly speaking, it is hardly an institutional theory at all.

Commons' common-sense analysis of organizations led him to at least the preliminaries of a humanistic analysis. Thus, his common-sense ground of interpretation led him directly to the role of purpose as the driving factor in human behaviour, and he tartly criticized Veblen for its neglect. In Veblen's (behaviouristic) analysis, he correctly observes, purposes 'turn out to be special cases of his general idea of institutional conduct', whereas in (Commons') 'institutional economics it is exactly this bias which we investigate as a part of the whole economic process'.[9] Then he very nicely proceeds to the consideration of the institution as a 'going concern' moulded by the 'working rules' (or procedures) imposed upon it by members who direct it in the light of their specific purposes. 'The Family, the Church, the Club, is a going concern, the transactions of its members are its going business, its working rules keep it going.'[10] All this sounds very like radical individualism and would be so if Commons could have extended it into unintended aspects of social

behaviour which forms the primary interest of that school. However, he restricts his analysis to that of the 'wanted' or 'intended'
consequences of action and gives no indication that he is aware of
the fact that collective action creates unintended consequences as
it becomes enmeshed in what Mitchell liked to call the 'logic of
the system'. His is a purely pragmatic theory.[11] 'I now define an
"institution" as collective action in control of individual action.
The rules, regulations, or bylaws I name the "rules of action" or
"working rules of collective action".'[12] And, 'This control of the
acts of one individual [by others] always *results in, and is
intended to result in*, a benefit to other individuals.'[13]

Working rules govern 'transactions' or the relations between
men. There are three basic types of transactions: (1) the rationing
transactions between policy-makers which are occupied with
laying down (the) working rules of other transactions; (2) mana-
gerial transactions which govern the relations between inferiors
and superiors; and (3) the bargaining transactions which pertain
to the transfer of property. These working rules, which govern the
forms of personal relations, and thus give character to collective
action, are in turn established through *negotiations* between
interested parties – compromises around a table of conflicting
interests, after the fashion of 'collective bargaining'.[14]

This is the image of the process of social change, collective bargaining over working rules is the process of social change; and it
is through the analysis of interested parties in conflict, yet in
compromise and settlement of the working rules for limited
periods of time, that collective action can be given its proper
place in economic thought. For obviously, the change in the
working rules, whether pertaining to property rights through litigation, or wages through collective bargaining, or hosts of other
elements in the economy, changes the workings of the economy,
and thus should be taken into account in economic theory. This
is the institutionalist contribution to economic theory in Commons' thinking – the recognition of changes in the working of
economic collectives through the process of 'negotiational
psychology':

For Adam Smith, individuals were like atoms; Karl Marx
made the whole of society his unit of investigation. Others
followed out mechanical or organic analogies. But what is

needed in economics is some unit which has parts and can be analyzed: one that has been the *deliberate construction of the human mind and will.*[15]

or:

Collective action proceeds, indeed, not from the intellectual logic of philosophers and economists, but from the arguments, debates, conferences, compromises (etc.) . . . among ordinary people themselves . . . (farmers, laborers, business men, etc.) . . . when forced or persuaded to consider their common interests. The psychology of this give-and-take process of con- ciliation and agreement may be termed negotiational psycho- logy, to distinguish it from the pleasure–pain psychology of the individualistic economists since the eighteenth century.[16]

An interesting example of what might have come out of Com- mons' basic analysis, as well as a precise example of why it did not, is provided in the closing pages of his *Legal Foundations of Capitalism*. In these pages he first distinguished between the 'behaviouristic' analysis characteristic of the physical sciences and the 'volitional', i.e. purposive, analysis of the social sciences. This leads him to postulate the difference between 'natural' and 'artificial' evolution in the two respective fields.[17] He then says:

Economic phenomena, as we know them, are the result of arti- ficial selection and not of natural selection. Their evolution is like that of a steam engine or a breed of cattle, rather than like that of a continent, monkey or tiger. If you watch how the steam engine evolved from John Watt in 1776 to the Mogul locomotive in 1923, you will see how economic institutions evolved. The steam engine evolved by studying the mechanisms of nature, experimenting with the parts, and then rearranging them, so that steam would act in two directions instead of one direction, as nature intended. So with the evolution of that pro- cess of behavior which we name political economy. The subject- matter is the habits, customs and ways of thinking of produ- cers, consumers, buyers, sellers, borrowers, lenders and all who engage in what we name economic transactions. The method has been the adoption of common rules applying to the simi- lar transactions of all who come within the same concern. If you watch the development of the credit system out of the customs of businessmen in buying and selling, borrowing and lending, and out of the customs of courts in deciding disputes, according to the changing common rules, you will see how political economy evolved.[18]

Now this is quite true, and what is more, it is vastly significant to both economic theory and social theory in general. To reverse Commons' statement, you cannot understand how economic institutions have come to be what they are, and hence what they might conceivably be in the future, unless you understand these 'habits, customs and ways of thinking', etc.; and this is particularly true of such institutions as, in his example, the 'credit system'. But in subsequent sentences of the paragraph Commons goes on to explain how these phenomena are to be understood as evolving to the place they are:

> The desirable customs were selected gradually by the courts, the undesirable customs were progressively eliminated as bad practices, and out of the whole came the existing economic process, a going concern, symbolized by a flux of prices, and operating to build up an artificial mechanism of rules of conduct, creating incorporeal and intangible property *quite different from the unguided processes of nature.*
>
> Thus a volitional or economic theory starts with the *purpose* for which the artificial mechanism in question was designed, fashioned and remodeled. . . .[19]

If one wishes to apply the type of analysis outlined by Commons in this statement to an understanding of his specific example, one can readily appreciate why this analysis leads down a blind alley. Thus, according to Commons, the 'credit system' evolved through its various forms through an appreciation of its disability, at various stages, to perform the 'purpose' for which it 'was designed'. Now the single most important fact to understand about the credit system, surely, is its capacity to produce money, some multiple of the existing stock of specie. This is the most important property of the system economically, legally, historically or whatever. But the fact is that while the credit system has been performing this function through the 'bank multiplier' for many centuries, it is only comparatively recently, certainly within the last two hundred years, that such a 'function' was even suspected. How then is it that through all these years people have been adjusting an institution in accordance with its performance of a function they do not so much as suspect? This illustration shows perhaps not so much the falsity of Commons' analysis as its naïveté, its lack of sophistication, its inherent 'uninterestingness'. There is perhaps a determinate connection between the (previously unsuspected) function of the credit system and the changes that take place in its working rules or procedures, but to say that these changes take place because of a reappraisal of the institution in the light of its purpose certainly constitutes an overly pragmatic interpretation of historical processes.

It is not necessary to pursue Commons' specific analysis of administrative organizations through these pages, since his insights and suggestions are readily available in his own works. Before closing this discussion, however, it should be noted that Commons' wing of institutionalism is largely responsible for that strange undercurrent of anti-theoretical animus in certain institutional literature. As Commons himself observed, 'I have no system, I have an administrative process.'[20] But for Commons this was a statement of fact, not, as some of his followers have implied, a methodological triumph.[21]

In conclusion, one cannot but think that Commons' life was more important than his writings. His influence in the world of affairs and on his students and colleagues was enormous. His place in economics is that of a minor, if rather heroic, defender of common sense at a time when Veblen and the other institutionalists were embracing scientism. A glimpse of the really remarkable man Commons was, is provided in the following paragraph from *Myself* written at the age of seventy:

. . . now I take myself seriously. I cannot work, I feel myself a failure in my own home. Why should I parade? Here I sit with only one child left out of six. My oldest served in the War, with honors for bravery from the English and Russian governments, but disappeared from my home in 1930, under a persecution mania. Four died in infancy. My wife, who for thirty years saved me from blunders or got me out of them, and who read and corrected all my manuscripts, has been gone six years. My sickliness from childhood has often knocked me out of my work and sent me wandering over the earth looking for something new. These culminated in this collapse, which began in 1930, and now I cannot travel any more but must sit at my window reading detective stories and looking out on beautiful Lake Mendota and distant hills, which, in their continuous change every hour of the day are my substitute for travel. Then, too, I have saved no money, and in these distressing times, with my relatives in need of help more serious than my own, I worry about that mortgage which apparently is greater than my home will sell for.

Commons was a man one would rather have known than read.[22]

10 Conclusion: Social Philosophy and Economics

The kind of grand theorizing indulged in by Veblen is now out of vogue. One can hardly imagine any of the major journals of economics, including Veblen's own *Journal of Political Economy*, now publishing any of his major articles. Editors and reviewers would find them rather pointless and, above all, not up to the putative standards of modern scientific inquiry. Veblen's theories are not obviously (mathematically) 'rigorous', nor are they clearly (statistically) 'testable'. It is a queer thing, when one thinks of it, that Veblen, himself so enamoured of the methods of the physical and biological sciences, would now find himself ruled out of court on these very grounds. The latest phase of 'the evolution of the scientific point of view', at least in economics, would not have pleased Veblen; yet it is the consistent expression of his deepest bias. Both in his own work and in his reception by (most) later economists, Veblen fell victim to the methodological emulation of the 'hard' sciences. That is an ultimate irony Veblen would have greatly enjoyed.

But while Veblen's particular case is mainly of historic interest, it illustrates a very real contemporary problem. It is not only Veblen that has been ruled out of economics, but social philosophy. And one may legitimately question the sense of this rule. The question is particularly relevant to this study. For it has been mainly a study in social philosophy rather than in social science, and if social philosophy is worthless, as the rule implies, then the study itself may fairly be said to be worthless on prima facie grounds. It is this prima facie question which is of concern here.

Hitherto, the phrase 'social theory' and social philosophy have both been used to describe Veblen's thought. Use of these somewhat ambiguous terms was deliberate. It leaves open the question of whether Veblen's 'theory' was essentially 'scientific' or 'philosophical'. Following Popper,[1] the distinction rests in the refutability of the theories. A scientific theory is refutable, a philosophic theory is not. The writer does not pretend to know which of these appellations best describes Veblen's theory. It is sometimes called social philosophy here in order to emphasize that *even if it is only philosophic*, in the sense of irrefutable, *it is still important*.

If a theory is irrefutable, what is the sense of discussing it? One irrefutable theory is apparently as good as another. Popper has shown the weakness in this argument. One may argue and believe that a theory is false even though one can never prove that it is:

> . . . every *rational* theory, no matter whether scientific or philosophical, is rational insofar as it tries to *solve certain problems*. A theory is comprehensible and reasonable only in its relation to a given *problem-situation*, and it can be rationally discussed only by discussing this relation.
>
> .   .   .
>
> Now if we look upon a theory as a proposed solution to a set of problems, then the theory immediately lends itself to critical discussion – even if it is nonempirical and irrefutable. For we can now ask questions such as, Does it solve the problem? Does it solve it better than other theories? Has it perhaps merely shifted the problem? Is the solution simple? Is it fruitful? Does it perhaps contradict other philosophic theories needed for solving other problems?
>
> Questions of this kind show that a critical discussion even of irrefutable theories may well be possible.[2]

Behaviourism is an example. Behaviourism cannot be refuted, but as the discussion in Chapter 7 has laboured to show, behaviourism contradicts the equally irrefutable theory of rationalism needed to account for important phenomena ranging from the problem of perception to social change.

Popper has emphasized the interconnections between philosophic and scientific theories:

> *Genuine philosophical problems are always rooted in urgent problems outside philosophy, and they die if these roots decay.*
> . . . there are others who do not feel this urge, who have no serious and pressing problem but who nevertheless produce

exercises in fashionable methods, and for whom philosophy is application (of whatever insight or technique you like) rather than *search*. They are luring philosophy into the bog of pseudo-problems and verbal puzzles; either by offering us pseudo-problems for real ones (the danger which Wittgenstein saw), or by persuading us to concentrate upon the endless and pointless task of unmasking what they rightly or wrongly take for pseudo-problems or 'puzzles' (the trap into which Wittgenstein fell).[3]

Popper emphasizes the importance of scientific problems to philosophy. According to this opinion, an equally strong case can be made for the importance of philosophic problems to social science. It may even be suggested that the most important theories in social science are, in fact, not scientific at all; they are irrefutable theories and hence, properly speaking, philosophic theories.

There are essentially two allegations here, however, and it is best to keep them separate. First, it is alleged that even if the important theories in social 'science' are refutable, they grow out of philosophic positions. Secondly, it is alleged that the most important social theories (even in such a social science as economics) are not refutable and are therefore philosophic.

The first allegation rests on this view: the social sciences create models which are based on certain assumptions. From these models are derived hypotheses which are tested. The assumptions are derived from philosophic theories.[4]

This interpretation flies in the face of two well-known positions in the history and methodology of economics: the alleged 'independence' of economic theory from philosophic thought associated with Joseph Schumpeter, and the alleged 'irrelevance' of the assumptions of economics associated with Milton Friedman. Each deserves extended treatment, but only the basic outlines can be presented here.

Schumpeter's position is not nearly as strong in the text of his *History of Economic Analysis* as the following citation implies. Indeed, much of that text seems to refute it, and since Schumpeter did not live to finish the manuscript, one will never know what his last word on the subject would have been. But the statement is a good expression of a commonly held belief and is cited in that sense, leaving the question of Schumpeter's final judgment open to question. He said that the effort to relate economic doctrines to philosophic schools is 'one of the most important sources of pseudo-explanations of the evolution of economic analysis'. These efforts, he continues, though they 'abound in the literature should be recognized ... for what they are – frills without importance that nevertheless obliterate the filiation of scientific ideas'. He arrives at the startling conclusion that 'even those economists that held very definite philosophic views ... were *as a matter of fact* not influenced by them when doing their work of analysis'.[5]

It is difficult to argue against this view precisely because if it means what it says, it is patently erroneous. One can hardly imagine the work of any major economist – including Schumpeter himself – without, for example, the assumption of a rational (in the sense of purposive) man. Thus, in order to defend Schumpeter's position, one must argue that the rational man is not a philosophic doctrine (for example, derived from, though not necessarily identical to, that envisaged in utilitarianism) but rather a *fact*. But if this were a fact, then behaviourism could be refuted (not merely considered false), and this has not been accomplished to the satisfaction of behaviourists – to say the very least.

Schumpeter has here fallen victim to a kind of myopia very common among economists. It is that the particular social philosophy used in the analysis seems so straightforward, so commonsensical, that it is not regarded as a social philosophy at all but rather as self-evident truth. A particularly striking instance of this naïveté is provided in the following pronouncement by L. M. Lackman:

> What entitles us to treat wants and resources as data and disinterest ourselves in their causal derivation is the simple fact that *qua* economists we have nothing to say about them. ... Expectations, on the other hand, are on a somewhat different plane as they are, while wants and resources are not, largely the result of the experience of economic processes.[6]

What this statement means is that Lackman has an (implicit) social theory which tells him that wants and resources are not the result of 'experience of economic processes'. Veblen, on the other hand (and Frank H. Knight for that matter – see Chapter 3 above), has an (explicit) social theory that they are. Thus, according to Lackman's social theory, Veblen would not be entitled to look at wants and resources '*qua* economist', while, by the same criterion, given Veblen's social theory, Veblen would. This is not to mention the problem of the criterion by which Lackman rules problems in or out of economics, nor the futility, indeed the intellectual destructiveness, of the attempt.

Until these obvious kinds of objections to the doctrine of the independence of philosophic and economic theories are met, further discussion of this (apparently) fallacious doctrine is pointless.

Milton Friedman's position is much more interesting.[7] The present position is that the relevance of social philosophy to economics lies largely in the assumptions. Friedman contends that the truth or falsity of the assumptions is irrelevant to economics! Clearly this is a bridge that one cannot permit to be burned.

Friedman contends that true predictions can be obtained from false assumptions. He also observes that true predictions do not necessarily imply true assumptions. In this he is, of course, absolutely correct. He is merely stating the error of two well-known logical fallacies: the fallacy of denying the antecedent, and the fallacy of affirming the consequent, respectively.[8] But his implication that this argues for the irrelevance of the assumptions is incorrect.

The reason for Friedman's error is most easily seen in connection with two *valid* rules of logic which are symmetrical with the above two fallacies. The first is *modus tollens*. It holds (in Friedman's phraseology) that if the predictions are false, then (in a logically valid theory) the assumptions are also false. This rule at least establishes a certain connection between prediction and assumption, but one which would perhaps not be appealing to Friedman. 'So what,' he may well say. 'All that we are interested in is prediction. If the predictions are false, that is what we want to know. The fact that the assumptions are also false is simply a curiosity.' This is a strong argument that can be countered by, of all things, an empirical consideration.

Just how many of the really important 'predictions' of economics are empirically testable? The fact is that almost *none* are. One of the most important, if not the most important, predictions of economics, for example, is that the perfectly competitive model will result in a state of Pareto optimality. This has never been empirically tested, nor can one imagine how it ever could be tested. From this important prediction others follow, such as that monopoly, technological externality, barriers to trade, etc., will prevent convergence to Pareto optimality. Yet these predictions too, so important to economic theory and economic policy, have never been empirically tested, nor can they be. Indeed, one may go so far as to say that these and many other problems that Friedman has himself worked on through his most productive life are similarly not testable in prediction. Are he and other economists to abandon their work simply because it is known *in advance* that their predictions will not be testable?

Certainly not, because the *assumptions* may be testable and, by the *valid* rule of *modus ponens*, true assumptions (in a logically valid theory) will yield true predictions. Thus, if one were to follow the implications of Friedman's methodology and pursue only those theories whose predictions are testable, one would have a very underpowered science. Testable hypotheses would be neglected simply because they are assumptions. This would not only drastically curb the empirical relevance of the science but, as argued above, would rule out of court most of the interesting problems and predictions of economics. The characteristic method of economics is, in fact, *modus ponens*.

Now the discussion has worked itself very much into a corner. If philosophic theories yield hypotheses which become assumptions in scientific theories (such as economics), and if these assumptions (hypotheses) are testable (refutable), then these are not philosophic theories at all, but rather scientific theories. For example, by *modus tollens*, refutation of the assumption in the scientific theory is identical to refutation of the hypothesis in the philosophic theory, which refutes that theory. Either apparently one denies the logical connection between the two kinds of theories or one denies the distinction; there is no half-way house.

It seems apparent that every scientific theory has a philosophic component, in itself irrefutable, yet necessary to establish logical connections between the scientific portions. Thus, there are no purely scientific theories (although there may be purely philosophic theories) – only parts of philosophic theories which are scientific. Further, progressive scientific knowledge consists at least partly in the attempt to increase the refutability of philosophic theories – to derive from these theories empirically testable consequences. Thus there is no immanent distinction between the two kinds of theory, for one will never know what theory will someday be testable. It also follows from this view that social science is largely a refutable 'expression' of philosophy. That is why a Veblen is so interesting, even from a scientific point of view and even where his theories are not refutable: they may someday be or through criticism they may lead to theories which are.

One may go even further and suggest that the rush towards mathematical expression and the emphasis on statistical techniques have together largely destroyed the ability to theorize freely, to generate new ideas and especially to communicate new discoveries through published journals and books. The medium has become more important than the message; scientism is destroying science in contemporary social theory. Perhaps a return to that grand theorizing represented both by Veblen and leaders in the traditional mainstream of economics would be a becoming remedy for that air of dismay, mentioned in the Introduction, in contemporary economics.[9]

Notes

Chapter 1

1. See Benjamin Ward, *What's Wrong with Economics?* (New York: Basic Books, 1972.)
2. Otto Nathan and Heinz Norden, *Einstein on Peace* (New York: Simon & Schuster, 1960) p. 322. The writer is indebted to William Dean Williams, 'The Mathematics of Veblenian Economics', unpublished Ph.D. dissertation (Union Graduate School, 1972) for this reference.
3. Cited in Joseph Dorfman, *Thorstein Veblen and his America*, rev. ed. (New York: Augustus M. Kelley, 1966) p. 349.
4. Thorstein Veblen, 'Mr Cummings' Strictures on *The Theory of the Leisure Class*', *Journal of Political Economy* (Dec 1899) pp. 106–17; republished in Leon Ardzrooni (ed.), *Essays in our Changing Order* (New York: Viking Press, 1943) p. 30.
5. In a 1931 letter cited in Dorfman, *Thorstein Veblen*, p. 507.
6. Joseph A. Schumpeter, *History of Economic Analysis* (London: Allen & Unwin, 1955) p. 470.
7. Paul T. Homan, 'The Institutional School', *Encyclopedia of the Social Sciences*, vol. v, p. 388.
8. Wesley C. Mitchell, 'The Prospects of Economics', in Rexford G. Tugwell (ed.), *The Trend of Economics* (New York: F. S. Crofts, 1930) pp. 17–18.
9. Wesley C. Mitchell, 'Commons on Institutional Economics', in Joseph Dorfman (ed.), *The Backward Art of Spending Money and Other Essays* (New York: McGraw-Hill, 1937) section vii.
10. Paul T. Homan, 'An Appraisal of Institutional Economics', paper presented at Round Table Conference on 'Institutional Economics', 1931, reported in *American Economic Review, Supplement* (Mar 1932) pp. 105–16; *American Economic Review* (Mar 1932) pp. 10–17:

> My correspondence and my reading once reached every well-known economist of supposed institutional proclivities, and they divide roughly into two classes: those who refuse to define institutional economics, and those whose definitions disagree. (p. 12)
>
> .   .
>
> There is, then, some point in the contention of Mr Dorfman, Veblen's biographer, that Veblen alone may be classified under the category of institutional economics. (p. 10)

11. D. R. Scott, 'Veblen not an Institutionalist', *American Economic Review* (June 1933) pp. 274-7. Scott has an excellent reason for his belief: 'To call him an institutional economist would emphasize an incidental aspect of his work rather than characterize its essential features.... His philosophic bias became that of a materialistic monist' (pp. 276-7).

12. Eric Roll, *A History of Economic Thought* (London: Faber & Faber, 1954) p. 454.

13. *Fortune* (Dec 1947) p. 133.

14. Thorstein Veblen, 'Why is Economics not an Evolutionary Science?', *Quarterly Journal of Economics* (July 1898) pp. 373–97; republished in Thorstein Veblen, *The Place of Science in Modern Civilization and Other Essays* (New York: Viking Press, 1919).

15. Strictly speaking, behaviourism is but the psychological wing of the more general philosophic positions of positivism or, better, 'scientism'. The latter concept is examined and criticized in F. A. Hayek, *The Counter-Revolution of Science* (New York: Free Press of Glencoe, 1964), a book which is 'required reading' for the present text. Behaviourism is used here to describe these positions because it is a better-known school and because the psychology of behaviourism is basic to the general position of positivism and scientism in social theory.

16. John Maynard Keynes, 'Francis Ysidro Edgeworth', in *Essays in Biography* (London: Mercury Books, 1961) p. 233.

Chapter 2

1. Thorstein Veblen, 'The Preconceptions of Economic Science', *Quarterly Journal of Economics*, Part I (Jan 1899), Part II (July 1899), Part III (Feb 1900); republished in *The Place of Science in Modern Civilization*, pp. 82–179.

2. Paul T. Homan, *Contemporary Economic Thought* (New York: Harper Bros., 1928) p. 107.

3. An excellent introduction to the German historical school may be found in Hermann Schumaker, 'The Historical School', *Encyclopedia of the Social Sciences*, vol. v, pp. 371–7.

4. See Eugen von Böhm-Bawerk, 'The Historical *vs.* the Deductive Method in Political Economics', *Annals of the American Academy of Political and Social Science* (Oct 1890) p. 249. In this article Böhm-Bawerk seemed prepared to compromise:

> If now, we put all misunderstandings aside, the *Status controversia* may be reduced to the following simple terms: the question is not whether the historical method or the exact [deductive] method is the correct one, but solely whether, alongside of the unquestionably warranted historical method of economics, we shall not recognize the 'isolating' method.

5. Cited in Dorman, *Thorstein Veblen*, pp. 17–18.

6. Statement by General Francis A. Walker, cited in Richard T. Ely, *Ground under our Feet* (New York: Macmillan, 1938) p. 127.

7. See the excellent discussion in Joseph Dorfman, *The Economic Mind in American Civilization* (New York: Viking Press, 1949) vol. III, pp. 92–110.

8. William Watts Folwell, 'The True Method in Political Economy', paper read before the Minnesota Academy of Natural Sciences, 5 Jan 1882, p. 7.

9. A copy of the original constitution of the society is included in Ely, *Ground under our Feet*, appendix III.

10. Ibid., p. 136.

11. Richard T. Ely, 'Discussion of the Platform at Saratoga' (Report of the Secretary on the Organization of the American Economic Association), *Publications of the American Economic Association*, I I (Mar 1896) 29.

12. Ibid., p. 21

13. Ely, *Ground under our Feet*, p. 137.

14. Ely, 'Discussion', pp. 21 ff.

15. Ely, *Ground under our Feet*, p. 141.

16. Ibid., p. 140.

17. American Economic Association, 'Constitution, Bylaws and Resolutions of the American Economic Association', *Supplement, American Economic Association Publications* (July 1889) p. 3.

18. Ibid., Resolution II, p. 7.

19. Henry C. Adams and others, *Science Economic Discussion* (New York: The Science Company, 1886).

20. E. J. James, 'The State as an Economic Factory', Ibid., p. 24.

21. Ely, 'Ethics and Economics', Ibid., pp. 54–5. Ely substantially qualified this view in response to Taussig's criticism that this makes it 'not a new school of political economy, but a new school as to something else'. F. W. Taussig, 'The State as an Economic Factor', ibid., p. 35. See also Richard T. Ely, *Outlines of Economics*, rev. ed. (New York: Macmillan, 1916) p. 69.

22. Henry C. Adams, 'Economics and Jurisprudence', in *Science Economic Discussion*, pp. 84–5.

23. Ely, 'Ethics and Economics', p. 154.

24. Richard T. Ely, 'The Past and the Present of Political Economy', *Johns Hopkins University Studies in Historical and Political Science* (Mar 1884) p. 9.

25. The most concise statement of the plans and programmes of the historical school is found in John K. Ingram's Preface to the English edition of Ely's *An introduction to Political Economy* (London: S. Sonnenschein, 1891) pp. 3–6. Ingram outlines the three positions stated here and advances a fourth – *'un grand dégel'*, a great thaw, from the barren ideas of the old science.

26. Frank A. Fetter, 'The Next Decade of Economic Theory', *Papers and Proceedings of the Thirteenth Annual Meeting of the American Economic Association* (Feb 1901) pp. 236–7. Seligman, one of the prime movers of the historical school, assented to this judgement, Ibid., pp. 249–250. See also Jacob H. Hollander, 'Economic Theorizing and Scientific

Progress', *American Economic Review, Supplement* (Mar 1969) p. 125; and Wesley C. Mitchell, *Lecture Notes on Types of Economic Theory* (New York: Augustus M. Kelley, 1949) vol. II, pp. 119–23.

27. Cited in Ely, *Ground under our Feet*, p. 150.

28. Frank A. Fetter, 'The Economists and the Public', *American Economic Review* (Mar 1925) p. 14. Freud detected a similar tendency in the early development of psychoanalysis. In response to Jung's mystical tendencies, Freud wrote:

> I therefore don once more my horn-rimmed paternal spectacles and warn my dear son to keep a cool head and rather not understand something than make such great sacrifices for the sake of understanding. I also shake my wise gray locks over the question of psychosynthesis and think: Well, that is how the young folks are; they really enjoy things only when they need not drag us along with them, where with our short breath and weary legs we cannot follow.

Letter, Freud to Jung, 16 April 1909, in C. G. Jung, *Memories, Dreams, Reflections* (New York: Vintage Books, 1963) p. 362.

29. Frank H. Knight, 'The Limitations of Scientific Method in Economics', in Tugwell (ed.), *The Trend of Economics*, pp. 249–50, citing Thorstein Veblen, 'Gustav Schmoller's Economics', *Quarterly Journal of Economics*, XVI (Nov 1901) 262; reprinted in *The Place of Science in Modern Civilization*, pp. 252–78:

> The 'natural laws' found by this means are necessarily of the nature of empiricism, colored by the bias or ideas of the investigator. The outcome is a body of aphoristic wisdom, perhaps beautiful and valuable after its kind, but quite fatuous measured by the standards and aims of modern science. As is well known, no substantial theoretic gain was made along this romantic-historical line of inquiry and speculation, for the reason apparently, that there are no cultural laws of the kind aimed at, beyond the unprecise generalities that are sufficiently familiar beforehand to all passably intelligent adults.

Knight later deplored the tendency to make him the 'devil' of institutionalism. He declared, 'I am in fact as "institutionalist" as anyone, in a positive sense. I diverge only in not damning "economics" in its essential meaning.' See 'Discussion', Kenneth E. Boulding, 'A New Look at Institutionalism', *American Economic Review* (May 1957) p. 12. In this paper Boulding spoke of Institutionalism in the past tense – as something which died out in the 1930s. This notwithstanding the fact that in his audience were several living, (hotly) breathing institutionalists!

30. Lionel Robbins, *An Essay on the Nature and Significance of Economic Science*, 2nd ed. (London: Macmillan, 1952) p. 83.

31. See also the discussion in Chapter 8 below.

32. Ludwig von Mises, *Human Action: A Treatise on Economics*, 3rd ed. (Chicago: Henry Regnery, 1966) p. 4. While the 'positivism' in this statement is precise, 'Darwinian evolution' should be substituted for 'Newtonian mechanics'. Since Mises regarded the historical school as positivism as well, his statement is open to interpretation.

Chapter 3

1. Wesley C. Mitchell, editor's introduction to *What Veblen Taught* (New York: Viking Press, 1936), included in Dorfman (ed.) *The Backward Art of Spending Money*, as 'Thorstein Veblen'.

2. David Riesman, *Thorstein Veblen* (New York: Charles Scribner's Sons, 1953). While not in the least attempting to deny a connection between thought and personality, or the interest of such studies (once it is agreed that they have nothing to do with the validity of an author's ideas), Riesman's 'interpretation' seems particularly far-fetched because of his evident inability to appreciate the substantive, intellectual problems faced by Veblen in the development of his theory. To give just one example, Riesman interprets Veblen's criticism of Marx and J. B. Clark in terms of a psychological revolt against a 'father figure'. Since Marx was the leading proponent of historicism and Clark the leading American mainstream economist, and since Veblen had to walk on a very narrow path between the two, it was absolutely necessary, *on intellectual grounds alone*, to criticize them.

3. The biographical material presented here is almost wholly contained in Dorfman's *Thorstein Veblen*. Other works on Veblen and the institutionalists are briefly discussed at the end of this chapter.

4. Lewis Mumford, 'Thorstein Veblen', *New Republic*, 5 August 1931, pp. 314–15. There is a vast range of opinion over the merits of Veblen's literary style. In the present opinion, Veblen was an unsurpassed master of the word, phrase, sentence, and occasionally even essay; but he was an absolutely miserable writer of books. This seems to be a common attribute of masters of the pungent phrase.

5. Ibid.

6. Cited in Mitchell, 'Thorstein Veblen', p. 289.

7. Dorfman, *Thorstein Veblen*, pp. 196–7.

8. Ibid., p. 500.

9. Max Lerner, editor's introduction to *The Portable Veblen* (New York: Viking Press, 1948) p. 31.

10. Veblen, 'Mr Cummings' Strictures on *The Theory of the Leisure Class*', p. 21.

11. Veblen, 'Why is Economics not an Evolutionary Science?', p. 70.

12. Dorfman, *Thorstein Veblen*, p. 57.

13. Ibid., p. 11.

14. Ibid. Much is rightly made of the cultural isolation in which Veblen was raised. He entered American civilization completely green – as that 'man from Mars' he so resembles in his writings. As Wesley C. Mitchell points out, in 'Thorstein Veblen', much of Veblen's brilliant essay on 'The Intellectual Pre-eminence of the Jews in Modern Europe' is autobiographical (as see below, Chapter 4). Thus, Veblen's observation, 'One who goes away from home will come to see many unfamiliar things, and to take note of them; but it does not follow that he will swear by all the

strange gods whom he meets along the road.' Ardrzooni (ed.), *Essays in our Changing Order*, p. 230.

15. Cited by Dorfman, *Thorstein Veblen*, p. 7.

16. Ibid., p. 12.

17. Ibid.

18. Ibid., pp. 30–1.

19. Ibid., pp. 31–3.

20. Ibid., p. 36.

21. The whole question of the influence of pragmatism and instrumentalism upon institutionalism is not examined here. This in spite of the fact that Veblen was not only a student of Pierce but also a colleague of Dewey, that Mitchell was a student and friend of Dewey, and that virtually all the institutionalists give Dewey credit as a source of inspiration. C. E. Ayres, indeed ranks Dewey with Veblen as a founder of institutionalism. Ayres, 'The Co-ordinates of Institutionalism', *American Economic Review* (May 1951) p. 47.

The reason, quite simply, is that instrumentalism is a much larger and in some ways more difficult subject than institutionalism itself. (See, e.g., the collection of essays in honour of Dewey entitled *The Philosopher of the Common Man* (New York: G. P. Putnam's Sons, 1940), especially the essays by Ernest Nagel, 'Reconstruction of Logical Theory', and Arthur F. Murphy, 'The Nature of Philosophy'.)

There is, in addition, the problem of the influence of Veblen on Dewey (see Dorfman, *Thorstein Veblen*, p. 450) which Dewey recognized. Thus, when one encounters a startling similarity in their views, especially in social theory (as, e.g., part II, chapter I of John Dewey, *Human Nature and Conduct* (New York: Henry Holt, 1922), the presumption is perhaps in favour of Veblen's precedence. This fact is too often overlooked by Veblen's reviewers, as in the case of Homan, *Contemporary Economic Thought*, p. III.

22. In a letter to J. Franklin Jameson (16 May 1883), Veblen wrote that he was taking 'Professor Sumner's two years' course of lectures on U.S. political and financial history' and that 'I have liked the lectures very much and think they have grown more interesting the farther they have gone on'. Cited in Dorfman, *Thorstein Veblen*, appendix I, p. 545.

23. From a letter written by Ellen Veblen, cited ibid., p. 57.

24. Ibid., p. 68.

25. Edward Bellamy, *Looking Backward* (New York: World Publishing Co., 1946) esp. pp. 117–18, 152–5, 264–9.

26. Dorfman, *Thorstein Veblen*, p. 255.

27. Ibid., p. 256.

28. Ibid. (Dorfman's parentheses).

29. Ibid.

30. Ibid., p. 257.

31. Ibid., p. 299.

32. Ibid.

33. Ibid., p. 269.

34. Ibid., p. 272.

35. Ibid., p. 306.

36. Ibid., p. 594.

37. Mitchell, 'Thorstein Veblen', p. 302. There was, however, a change in emphasis in the first decade of this century (see Chapter 5 below).

38. Veblen mentioned his work on this book in a letter to 'Mrs Gregory' (27 June 1903). He wrote:

> You may have seen enough to criticize in the pamphlet ['The Use of Loan Credit in Modern Business']... but the book, I am credibly told, is still more 'beyond', or as my friends who have seen it say, beside the point. Its name is the *Theory of Business Enterprise* – a topic on which I am free to theorize with all the abandon that comes of immunity from the facts.

Cited in Dorfman, *Thorstein Veblen*, pp. 219–20.

39. Irving Fisher, Capital and Interest', *Political Science Quarterly* (Sep 1909) p. 513.

40. See Lerner, *The Portable Veblen*, p. 7.

Chapter 4

1. The selections in this section are from Thorstein Veblen, 'Some Neglected Points in the Theory of Socialism', *Annals of the American Academy of Political and Social Science* (Nov 1891) pp. 345–63; republished in *The Place of Science in Modern Civilization*.

2. Thorstein Veblen, *The Theory of the Leisure Class*.

3. John Kenneth Galbraith, *The Affluent Society* (New York: New American Library, 1958) p. 51.

4. Kenneth Boulding, 'Economics as a Moral Science', *American Economic Review*, LIX (Mar 1969) 2.

5. Thorstein Veblen, 'The Socialist Economics of Karl Marx and his Followers', *Quarterly Journal of Economics* (Aug 1906) pp. 578–95; (Feb 1907) pp. 299–322; republished in *The Place of Science in Modern Civilization*.

6. Thorstein Veblen, 'On the Intellectual Pre-eminence of the Jews in Modern Europe', *Political Science Quarterly* (Mar 1919) pp. 33–42; republished in Ardzrooni (ed.), *Essays in our Changing Order*.

Chapter 5

1. In the light of the thesis presented in Chapter 7 below, Veblen's choice of Menger and the Austrian school for attack becomes perhaps one of his greatest, although completely unintended, jokes.

2. Veblen, 'Why is Economics not an Evolutionary Science?', pp. 73–4.

3. Ibid., p. 74.

4. John Stuart Mill, *Autobiography* (New York: Henry Holt, 1887) p. 142. Veblen rather grudgingly admitted that Mill did not fit his stereotype. See 'The Preconceptions of Economic Science', pp. 151–3.

5. Thorstein Veblen, 'The Limitations of Marginal Utility', pp. 235–45.

6. Ibid., pp. 237–8 (author's italics).

7. Ibid., p. 235, n. 2 (author's italics).

8. Ibid., p. 240.

9. This theme is re-examined in Chapter 7 below.

10. Thorstein Veblen, *The Instinct of Workmanship and the State of the Industrial Arts* (New York: B. W. Huebsch, 1914) p. 9.

11. Ibid., p. 3.

12. Ibid. p. 9.

13. Veblen, *The Theory of the Leisure Class*, p. 15 (author's italics).

14. Mitchell (ed.), *What Veblen Taught*, p. 24. For example, while every man wants food, there is no food 'instinct'. The desire for food emerges from the energy requirements of the body (the 'unit characters').

15. Veblen notes that it is important 'to take note of how and with what effect the several instinctive proclivities cross, blend, overlap, neutralize or reinforce one another'. Veblen, *The Instinct of Workmanship*, pp. 8–9.

16. Veblen, 'The Place of Science in Modern Civilization', p. 6. The idle curiosity must be instinctive and more or less incorruptible in that while certain social pressures may affect its operation, or stop it altogether, the relaxation of these pressures will allow it to resume operation uninhibited and with no residual effects from the suppression. The reasons for this requirement become apparent with the discussion of the 'technological dynamic'.

17. Ibid., p. 9.

18. Ibid., p. 19. This statement may be viewed as a backhand to Dewey and James.

The concept of the idle curiosity is especially well set forth in Norman Kaplan's essay, 'Idle Curiosity', in Douglas F. Dowd (ed.), *Thorstein Veblen: A Critical Reappraisal* (Ithaca, N.Y.: Cornell Univ. Press, 1958). Its philosophic history is treated in Stanley M. Daugert's excellent *The Philosophy of Thorstein Veblen* (New York: King's Crown, 1950). To the latter's very stimulating discussion the writer owes an appreciation of the deep significance of Veblen's early paper on 'Kant's *Critique of Judgment*' (in Ardzrooni (ed.), *Essays in our Changing Order*) to his subsequent work. Veblen began, in this paper, to struggle with the differences between what later became the 'idle curiosity' and the 'habits of thought' – perhaps his most important distinction. This distinction is paralleled in many respects in his treatment of Kant's 'reflective judgment' and 'principle of adaptation'. The habits of thought are no doubt akin to Pierce's early 'guiding principles'. Veblen's early discussion of Kant's 'principle of adaptation' (p. 189) may be taken as a good description of what was later to become 'the idle curiosity':

The mind is unsatisfied with things until it can see how they belong together. The principle of adaptation says that the particular things do belong together, and sets the mind hunting to find out how. The principle of adaptation says that, in order to perform the normal action of the faculties, things must be conceived to be so co-ordinated in their action as to make up an organized whole ... what the principle of adaptation does for us is, therefore, in the first place, that it makes us guess, and that it guides our guessing. If it were not that we are dissatisfied with our knowledge so long as it remains in the shape of a mere manifold, we should never seek to get beyond a congeries of things in time and space; and, if it were not that the principle of adaptation shows us what we are to seek further, we should never find anything further in our knowledge.

19. It is significant that Veblen's specific discussion of instincts in his treatise on social theory, *The Instinct of Workmanship*, occupies only the *introduction*; this, as though to say that the real business at hand is the explanation of the evolution of habits of thought.

20. Thorstein Veblen, 'The Evolution of the Scientific Point of View', p. 40.

21. Veblen uses the term 'institution' in a variety of different ways. See Daugert, *The Philosophy of Thorstein Veblen*, pp. 49–51, and the discussion in Chapter 7 below.

22. Thorstein Veblen, *Absentee Ownership* (New York: B. W. Huebsch, 1923) p. 101, n. 1.

23. Veblen, *The Instinct of Workmanship*, pp. 147–8.

24. Thorstein Veblen, 'Industrial and Pecuniary Employments', in *The Place of Science in Modern Civilization*, p. 314.

25. Veblen, 'The Limitations of Marginal Utility', p. 239.

26. In the words of Joseph Schumpeter, 'Here, then, we have the propeller [technology] which is responsible first of all for economic and, in consequence of this, for any other social change, a propeller the action of which does not itself require any impetus external to it.' Joseph A. Schumpeter, 'Karl Marx', in *Ten Great Economists* (London: Allen & Unwin, 1956) p. 13.

27. Thorstein Veblen, *The Nature of Peace*, p. 197.

28. These stages and their interpretation are most conveniently presented in Veblen, 'The Place of Science in Modern Civilization'.

29. Veblen contends that the question of peace is not so much a question of fighting but of the fighting spirit. 'The point in question is not as to the occurrence of combat, occasional or sporadic, or even more or less frequent and habitual; it is a question as to the occurrence of an habitual bellicose frame of mind – a prevalent habit of judging facts and events from the point of view of the fight.' Veblen, *The Theory of the Leisure Class*, p. 15.

30. Veblen, 'The Socialist Economics of Karl Marx', p. 442.

31. Mitchell, 'Thorstein Veblen', p. 310.

32. Veblen, 'The Limitations of Marginal Utility', pp. 241–2.

Chapter 6

1. C. E. Ayres, *The Theory of Economic Progress* (Chapel Hill: Univ. of North Carolina Press, 1944) p. 95.
2. Ibid., pp. 73–4.
3. Ibid., pp. 95–6.
4. C. E. Ayres, 'The Co-ordinates of Institutionalism', *American Economic Review* (May 1951) p. 48.
5. Ibid., p. 49.
6. Ayres, *The Theory of Economic Progress*, p. 177 (author's italics).
7. Ibid., pp. 169–70. The reference in this citation is to Frank H. Knight, 'Intellectual Confusion in Morals and Ethics', *International Journal of Ethics*, XLV, pp. 208–9. The 'cultural lag' may be a real phenomenon, but it can only be interpreted as some cultural sectors (e.g. property rights) lagging behind other cultural sectors (business enterprise or the scientific-technological establishment) in a process of adjustment. Otherwise the lag becomes a human element as discussed in the next paragraph.
8. Ibid., pp. 111–12 (author's italics). As to 'Beethoven's quartets', see immediately below.
9. Ibid., p. 131. 'When people stay put in any particular locality things accumulate, and the accumulation of the *physical instruments* and materials of living constitutes a forcing bed of technological development' (author's italics).
10. Ibid., p. 118 (author's italics).
11. Ibid., p. 143. Ships, apparently, were not only a necessary but also a sufficient condition to the age of discovery. Otherwise the example would obviously be trivial.
12. Ibid., p. 211.
13. Ibid., p. 123.
14. Ibid., p. 118. Compare Veblen's quasi-rationalist, very cautious formulation of the technological dynamic: 'The larger the available body of information of this (impersonal matter-of-fact) character, and the more comprehensive and unremitting the share taken by the discipline of the machine process in the routine of daily life therefore, the greater, other things being equal, will be the rate of advance in the technological mastery of mechanical facts.' Veblen, *The Instinct of Workmanship*, p. 242.
15. Ayres, 'The Co-ordinates of Institutionalism', p. 51.
16. Morris A. Copeland, 'Psychology and the Natural Science Point of View', in Chandler Morris (ed.), *Fact and Theory in Economics* (Ithaca, N.Y.: Cornell Univ. Press, 1958). This discussion is limited to this one essay and is not meant to bear upon Copeland's other – many admirable – works. Indeed the difference between his methodological prescriptions and his specific analyses is a significant fact in itself. All the following citations are from this article.

Chapter 7

1. Wesley C. Mitchell, 'Bentham's Felicific Calculus', in Dorfman (ed.), *The Backward Art of Spending Money*, p. 127 (author's italics).
2. The term 'radical individualism' is chosen over such designations as, e.g., 'methodological individualism', not because it is necessarily a better term, nor because the present discussion is intended to be fundamentally different from the analysis of Hayek, Popper and other members of this school, but from a desire to avoid imputing responsibility to them for what may turn out to be a private opinion. This is necessary because of the incipient state of development of the theory. The debt owed by the writer to the published work of these theorists, and to the lectures given by Professor Popper and Dr J. Agassi at the London School of Economics, is evident in these pages.
3. Veblen, 'Why is Economics not an Evolutionary Science?', p. 78.
4. Cited in F. A. Hayek, *The Counter-Revolution of Science: Studies on the Abuse of Reason* (London: Collier-Macmillan, 1955) p. 83.
5. Karl R. Popper, *The Poverty of Historicism* (New York: Harper & Row, 1964) p. 65. See also Karl R. Popper, 'Towards a Rational Theory of Tradition', *Rationalist Annual* (1949) pp. 40–2.
6. Hayek, *The Counter-Revolution of Science*, p. 80.
7. Knight, 'The Limitations of Scientific Method in Economics', in Tugwell (ed.), *The Trend of Economics*, pp. 262–3.
8. As argued in Chapter 9 below, John R. Commons was particularly susceptible to the pragmatic interpretation.
9. Popper, *The Poverty of Historicism*, Preface, pp. vi–viii.
10. Popper, however, believes that a historicist would accept (1) but that (2) requires further proof. Ibid., pp. vi–viii.
11. The word 'thoughts' is placed in inverted commas because Watson denied the existence of thought and attributed what others describe as 'thinking' to movements of muscles in the throat.

Anyone who has attempted to follow out the convoluted lines of behaviouristic 'reasoning' cannot fail to appreciate the humour and pathos of these lines from a great contemporary novel. The foremost intellectual of a new revolutionary state is expected to tell the world: 'We are happy and proud to march with the masses. Blind matter regains the use of its eyes and knocks off the rosy spectacles which used to adorn the long nose of so-called thought. Whatever I have thought and written in the past, one thing is clear to me now; no matter to whom they belong, two pairs of eyes looking at a boot see the same boot, since it is identically reflected in both: and further, that the larynx is the seat of thought so that the working of the mind is a kind of gargling.' Vladimir Nabokov, *Bend Sinister* (London: Transworld Publishers, 1962) p. 140.
12. Discussion of 'Humanistic Behaviorism', *The Humanist* (May–June 1971) p. 35.
13. Horace M. Kallan, 'Behaviorism', *Encyclopedia of the Social*

Sciences, vol. II, p. 495. See also J. B. Watson, *Behaviourism* (London: Kegan Jaul, Trench, Trubner, 1931) esp. chap. 11; B. F. Skinner, *Contingencies of Reinforcement: A Theoretical Analysis* (New York: Appleton-Century-Crofts, 1969).

14. 'Humanistic Behaviorism', p. 35.

15. F. A. Hayek, *The Sensory Order: An Inquiry into the Foundations of Theoretical Psychology* (Chicago: Univ. of Chicago Press, 1972) p. 28. See also Solomon E. Asch, 'Gestalt Theory', *International Encyclopedia of the Social Sciences*, vol. VI, pp. 158–75.

16. Hayek, *The Counter-Revolution of Science*, p. 24.

17. Bertrand Russell, 'What is the Soul', in *Let the People Think* (London: Rationalist Press, 1961) pp. 111–12.

18. Veblen, 'The Preconceptions of Economic Science', p. 155.

19. As Veblen well realized; see Ibid., pp. 155–6, and Chapter 4 above.

20. Böhm-Bawerk, 'The Historical *vs.* the Deductive Method in Political Economy p. 260. The citation is, of course, in respect to the inductive programmes of the historical school. The reader will note that the criticisms advanced here against behaviourism are substantially the same as those advanced by Popper against inductivism. The same basic criticism is applicable to the two schools because methodologically they are substantially the same. They both wish to start with a 'clean slate' and restrict themselves only to observable phenomena. They equally question the 'propriety' or 'legitimacy' of the origins of hypothesis. Thus, inductivists cannot 'stand' mere speculative guesses; behaviourists are equally antipathetic to introspective-subjective methods. They both represent an attempt to obtain something more 'substantial' for hypothesis to be 'based upon'. They thus go hand in hand to a common doom with the problem of perception and meaning.

21. von Mises, *Human Action*, pp. 17–18. (The order of these statements has been slightly rearranged.)

22. Robbins, *An Essay on the Nature and Significance of Economic Science*, p. 157.

23. Walton H. Hamilton, 'Institution', *Encyclopedia of the Social Sciences*, vol. III, p. 84.

24. See also the discussion of habit immediately below.

25. It may be observed that the process of social change in this interpretation is analogous to the hypothetical-deductive method of science associated with the works of Karl R. Popper. Ideas are created and tested, the refutation of old ideas provides a stimulus to the discovery of new ideas, which are again tested. Similarly, new ideas arise, they create a social impact through technology or simply by influencing people's thinking and, thus, actions. The social impact of these ideas renders established procedures obsolete and provides a stimulus to adoption of new procedures. With change in procedures, the institutional structure necessarily adjusts, thereby affecting the viability of other more distant procedures, and so on 'world without end'.

26. For a graphical presentation of this 'cultural revolution', see Paul W. Barkley and David W. Seckler, *Economic Growth and Environmental*

Decay: The Solution Becomes the Problem (New York: Harcourt Brace Jovanovich, 1972) appendix A, p. 82.

27. See C. G. Beer, 'Instinct', *International Encyclopedia of the Social Sciences*, vol. VII, pp. 363–72; also Ronald Fletcher, *Instinct in Man* (New York: Schocken Books, 1966).

28. See Hayek, *The Sensory Order*, and Nicholas Georgescu-Roegen, 'Utility', *International Encyclopedia of the Social Sciences*, vol. XVI, pp. 236–67. The latter is particularly recommended for those who like to think of utility as a simple nineteenth-century concept.

29. Veblen, 'The Preconceptions of Economic Science', p. 156.

30. For example, it is by now obvious that the myth of the 'peasant farmer', caught up in his traditional ignorance, has been decisively refuted by the spread of agricultural technology.

31. 'Is it possible for a man to move the earth? Yes; but he must first find out another earth to stand upon.' Jeremy Bentham, *An Introduction to the Principles of Morals and Legislation* (Oxford: Basil Blackwell, 1948) p. 129.

Appendix

1. The manuscript of this book was substantially complete when the writer encountered Karl R. Popper's essay, 'Of Clouds and Clocks' reprinted in *Conjectures and Refutations: The Growth of Scientific Knowledge* (London and New York: Basic Books, 1962). This short appendix has been added to convey Popper's perceptive elucidation of the free will versus determinism, humanism versus behaviourism, problem and to suggest a possible avenue of further investigation on the subject.

2. Although Veblen at least brushed by one of the early critics of determinism, Charles Sanders Pierce at Johns Hopkins. See Popper, Ibid., pp. 212–14.

3. Cited Ibid., p. 218.

4. M. Schlick, cited Ibid., p. 227.

5. Ibid., p. 228.

6. Ibid., p. 247.

7. From this point on the discussion departs in some degree from that of Popper.

8. There is another interesting implication of this example. If the object being pursued is not a ball but, say, a rabbit, then obviously the optimal pursuit technique shifts over to that used by the dog. Of course, in such circumstances the man will adopt the same technique. The dog is unable to differentiate between choosing and non-choosing phenomena. This is a property he apparently shares with behaviourists.

Chapter 8

1. Lucy Sprague Mitchell, *Two Lives: The Story of Wesley Clair Mitchell and Myself* (New York: Simon & Schuster, 1953) pp. 80-1.
2. Ibid., p. 87.
3. Ibid., p. 90.
4. Ibid., p. 93.
5. Ibid., p. 92.
6. Ibid., pp. 176-7.
7. Ibid., p. 180.
8. Ibid., p. 527.
9. Ibid., p. 180.
10. Ibid., p. 527.
11. Ibid., pp. 534-5.
12. Wesley C. Mitchell, 'Bentham's Felicific Calculus', in Dorfman (ed.), *The Backward Art of Spending Money*, p. 177.
13. Mitchell, 'Postulates and Preconceptions of Economic Science', Ibid., p. 214.
14. Mitchell, 'Intelligence and the Guidance of Economic Evolution', Ibid., p. 116.
15. Mitchell, 'Postulates and Preconceptions of Economic Science', Ibid., p. 210.
16. Mitchell, 'Economics, 1904-1929', Ibid., p. 406.
17. Mitchell, 'Intelligence and the Guidance of Economic Evolution', Ibid., p. 117.
18. Mitchell, 'Thorstein Veblen', Ibid., p. 301 (author's italics).
19. Mitchell, 'The Role of Money in Economic Theory', Ibid., p. 171, citing J. Bonar (ed.), *Letters of Ricardo to Malthus* (Oxford, 1887) p. 18.
20. Cited in Wesley C. Mitchell, *Business Cycles*, 2nd ed. (New York: National Bureau of Economic Research, 1927) p. 59, n. 1 (translation of Löwe's comments by Mitchell in the same place).
21. Ibid., p. 59.
22. Wesley C. Mitchell, 'Quantitative Analysis in Economic Theory', Presidential Address delivered at the Thirty-seventh Annual Meeting of the American Economic Association, Dec 1924, in Dorfman (ed.), *The Backward Art of Spending Money*, p. 23.
23. Ibid., p. 21.
24. Ibid., p. 33.
25. Cited by Mitchell from *Schmollers Jahrbuch* for June 1926, in American Economic Association 'Round Table Discussion' on 'The Present Status and Future Prospects of Quantitative Economics', *American Economic Review, Supplement* (Mar 1928) p. 39.
26. Mitchell, 'Quantitative Analysis in Economic Theory', pp. 28-9.
27. American Economic Association, 'The Present Status and Future Prospects of Quantitative Economics' (Viner's comments), p. 31.
28. Ibid., p. 32.

29. Ibid.

30. Ibid., pp. 32–3.

31. Ibid., p. 33.

32. Ibid., p. 34 (author's italics).

33. Ibid. (Mitchell's comments), p. 40.

34. Ibid. (Black's comments), p. 44.

35. Mitchell, appendix to 'Quantitative Analysis in Economic Theory', pp. 37–41.

36. Wesley C. Mitchell, *Lecture Notes on Types of Economic Theory* (New York: Augustus M. Kelley, 1949) vol. II, p. 230.

37. 'Round Table Discussion' on 'The Use of the Quantitative Method in the Study of Economic Theory', *American Economic Review, Supplement* (Mar 1927) p. 20. The citation is from the minutes of the chairman, Holbrook Woking.

38. Mitchell, 'The Prospects of Economics', in Dorfman (ed.), *The Backward Art of Spending Money*, p. 25.

39. Ibid., p. 24.

40. Mitchell, 'Economics, 1904–1929', Ibid., p. 408 (writer's italics).

41. Mitchell, 'The Role of Money in Economic Theory', Ibid., p. 175.

Chapter 9

1. John Rogers Commons, *Myself* (New York: Macmillan, 1934). This book is one of the neglected classics of autobiography. It seems that in these last years of his life Commons discovered the literary style he needed, but never found, in his earlier works. Commons had a very concrete mind, and when he turned away from conceptualization to the personal narrative form, he had few equals. Except where otherwise indicated, the following autobiographical citations are from this work.

2. Selig Perlman, 'John Rogers Commons', in Commons, *The Economics of Collective Action*, ed. Kenneth H. Parsons (New York: Macmillan, 1950) p. 2.

3. John R. Commons, *Institutional Economics: Its Place in Political Economy* (Madison: Univ. of Wisconsin Press, 1959) p. 1.

4. Commons, *The Economics of Collective Action*, p. 14.

5. Ibid., p. 113.

6. Commons, *Institutional Economics*, pp. 101–2.

7. Ibid., p. 8.

8. Ibid., p. 5.

9. Ibid., pp. 654–5.

10. John R. Commons, *The Legal Foundations of Capitalism* (New York: Macmillan, 1924) p. 15.

11. Morris A. Copeland observes, 'His [Commons'] is a theory of economic planning by selection of the best existing practices. If one's task is only to select the best from a group of houses already built, a somewhat limited

investigation of theory and facts of house construction may suffice.' 'Social Evolution and Economic Planning', in Morris (ed.), *Fact and Theory in Economics*, p. 10.

12. Commons, *The Economics of Collective Action*, p. 26.

13. Commons, *Institutional Economics*, p. 70.

14. See Commons, *The Economics of Collective Action*, p. 23.

15. Ibid., p. 118 (author's italics).

16. Ibid., pp. 28–9.

17. Commons, *The Legal Foundations of Capitalism*, pp. 374–5.

18. Ibid., pp. 376–7.

19. Ibid., p. 377 ('purpose' Commons' italics, others the writer's).

20. An oral remark cited in Dorfman, *The Economic Mind in Amercan Civilization*, vol. IV, p. 390.

21. See Nathan L. Silverstein, 'An Appraisal of Institutional Economics: Comment', *American Economic Review* (June 1932) pp. 268–9.

22. See also David Seckler, 'The Naïveté of John R. Commons', *Western Economic Journal*, IV, 3 (Summer 1966) 261–7. The writer would like to take this opportunity to retract the tone if not the content of the article. It was written in response to excessive claims for Commons by certain of his disciples and was perhaps conditioned by a lingering resentment over having been forced to read, in preparation of this chapter, several thousand pages of Commons' writings (which seem to be organized by means of the random walk) in order to obtain what would constitute a good small book.

Chapter 10

1. Karl R. Popper, 'On the Status of Science and of Metaphysics', *Ratio*, I (1958) 97–115; reprinted in *Conjectures and Refutations: The Growth of Scientific Knowledge*, op. cit., pp. 184–200.

2. Ibid., p. 199.

3. Karl R. Popper, 'The Nature of Philosophic Problems and their Parts in Science', first published in the *British Journal for the Philosophy of Science*, III (1952) 72; reprinted in *Conjectures and Refutations*, pp. 66–96.

4. The connection between social science and philosophy is particularly close with respect to the 'behavioural assumptions' of the latter. 'It is probably no exaggeration to say that every important advance in economic theory during the last hundred years was a further step in the consistent application of subjectivism.' Hayek, *The Counter-Revolution of Science*, p. 31.

5. Schumpeter, *History of Economic Analysis*, p. 32.

6. L. M. Lackman, 'The Role of Expectation in Economics as a Social Science', *Economica* (Feb 1943) p. 12.

7. Milton Friedman, 'The Methodology of Positive Economics', in

Essays in Positive Economics (Chicago: Univ. of Chicago Press, 1953) pp. 3–43. The following may be an overly simple statement of Friedman's complete position. Since the writer is not 'positive' that he knows what Friedman 'really means' in this essay, he would not object to these remarks being interpreted as a criticism of a popular interpretation of Friedman's position.

8. Formally, these and subsequently used rules can be written (see Irving M. Copi, *Symbolic Logic* (New York: Macmillan, 1967) pp. 22–4):

Valid		*Invalid*	
Modus Tollens:	$A \supset B$	Fallacy of Denying the Antecedent:	$A \supset B$
	$\sim B$		$\sim A$
	$\therefore \sim A$		$\therefore \sim B$
Modus Ponens:	$A \supset B$	Fallacy of Affirming the Consequent:	$A \supset B$
	A		B
	$\therefore B$		$\therefore A$

9. Myron E. Sharpe has invented another name for this kind of economics in the title of his excellent book, *John Kenneth Galbraith and the Lower Economics* (White Plains, N.Y.: International Arts and Sciences Press, 1973). Whatever it is called, Sharpe agrees that economics needs more of it. Borrowing a phrase from Benjamin Ward, Sharpe says, 'The lower economics is institutional economics, and it possesses its own method, which has been aptly called storytelling.'

In reflecting on the great post-war rise of 'formalism' in economics, Ward concludes, '. . . dramatically new ideas are just not there. It is as if the interwar economists had some sort of uncanny ability to intuit the features that are now being traced out in more detail. The great methodological puzzle in economics is why a great methodological revolution should make so little substantive difference.' Ward, *What's Wrong with Economics?*, pp. 43–4.

Index

cial theory, 37–46, 56–63, 132, 136; 'split personality', x–xi, 7–9, 52–6, 61; as behaviourist, 54–55, 61–2, 66, 67, 83–5, 126; as humanist, 52–3, 85–6, 90; and stages of development, 63–7, 108; status, 2; style, x, 2, 22, 24, 143; works by, 33–5; works on, 35–6
Veblen effects, 45
Viner, Jacob, 111–14

Wallas, Graham, xiii, 2, 31
Watson, J. B., 8, 82
Winsconsin, University of, 19, 121–122
Wittgenstein, Ludwig, 134
Wolfe, A. D., 3

Yale University, 29
Young, Allyn A., ix, 30

Zionism, 49–51

Sept. 1981
Durham, N.C.